DIXIELAND JAZZ BANJO

Authentic Lead Sheets with Chord Diagrams
for Tenor & Plectrum Banjo

ARRANGED BY CHAD JOHNSON

ISBN 978-1-4803-6114-0

HAL•LEONARD®
CORPORATION

7777 W. BLUEMOUND RD. P.O. BOX 13819 MILWAUKEE, WI 53213

Visit Hal Leonard Online at
www.halleonard.com

CONTENTS

6	After You've Gone	62	Honeysuckle Rose
8	Ain't Misbehavin'	64	I Got Rhythm
3	Ain't She Sweet	66	In a Shanty in Old Shanty Town
10	Alabama Jubilee	69	Ja-Da
14	Alabamy Bound	72	The Jazz-Me Blues
18	Alexander's Ragtime Band	76	Lazy River
24	At Sundown	78	Mississippi Mud
26	Avalon	84	My Baby Just Cares for Me
28	Baby Face	86	My Blue Heaven
32	Basin Street Blues	81	My Honey's Loving Arms
34	Bei Mir Bist Du Schon (Means That You're Grand)	88	Original Dixieland One-Step
38	Bill Bailey, Won't You Please Come Home	92	Royal Garden Blues
42	Blue Skies	98	St. Louis Blues
21	Breezin' Along with the Breeze	102	Some of These Days
44	Bye Bye Blackbird	104	Somebody Stole My Gal
46	Bye Bye Blues	106	Stompin' at the Savoy
48	California, Here I Come	95	Struttin' with Some Barbecue
50	Chinatown, My Chinatown	108	Summertime
52	'Deed I Do	110	Sweet Georgia Brown
55	Dinah	118	That's a Plenty
58	Do You Know What It Means to Miss New Orleans	112	'Way Down Yonder in New Orleans
		114	The World Is Waiting for the Sunrise
60	Georgia on My Mind	116	Yes Sir, That's My Baby

Ain't She Sweet

Words by Jack Yellen
Music by Milton Ager

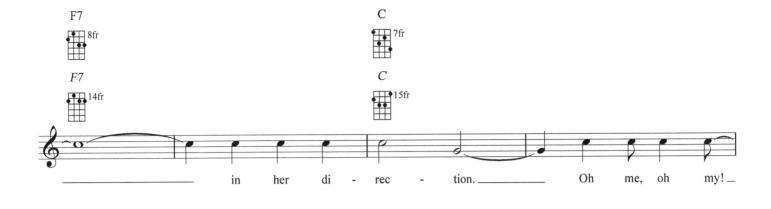

in her di - rec - tion. _____ Oh me, oh my! _

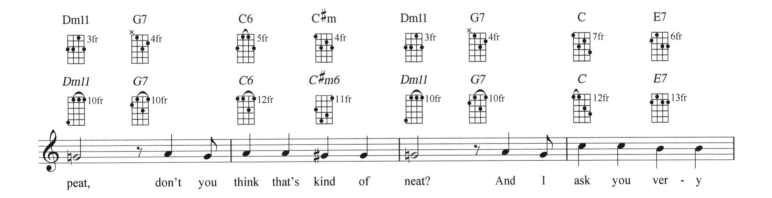

Ain't that per - fec - tion? _____ I re -

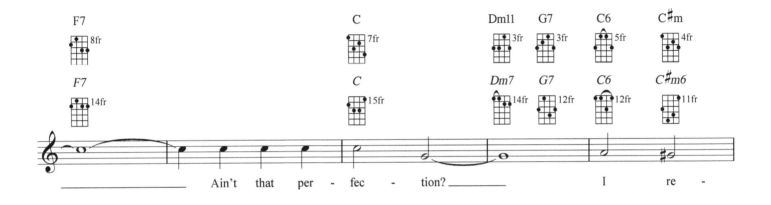

peat, don't you think that's kind of neat? And I ask you ver - y

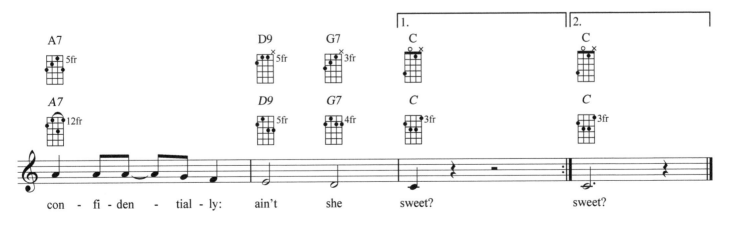

con - fi - den - tial - ly: ain't she sweet? sweet?

After You've Gone

from ONE MO' TIME

Words by Henry Creamer
Music by Turner Layton

Ain't Misbehavin'

from AIN'T MISBEHAVIN'
Words by Andy Razaf
Music by Thomas "Fats" Waller and Harry Brooks

Your kiss - es are worth wait - in' for, be - lieve me.

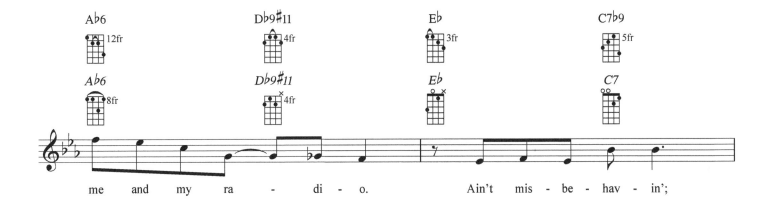

I don't stay out late, don't care to go. I'm home a - bout eight, just

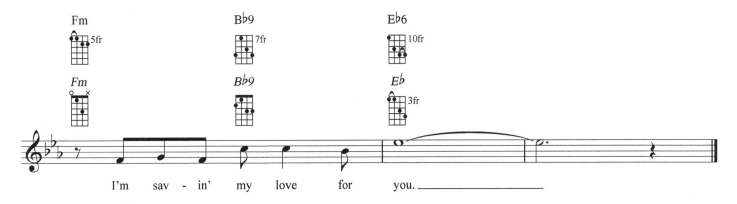

me and my ra - di - o. Ain't mis - be - hav - in';

I'm sav - in' my love for you. _____

Alabama Jubilee

Words by Jack Yellen
Music by George Cobb

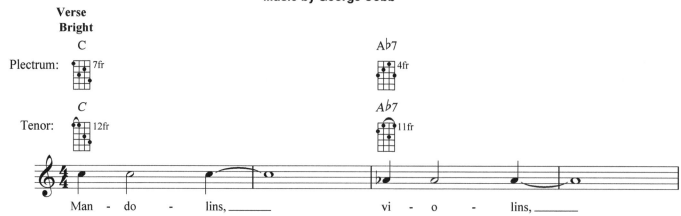

Man - do - lins, _____ vi - o - lins, _____

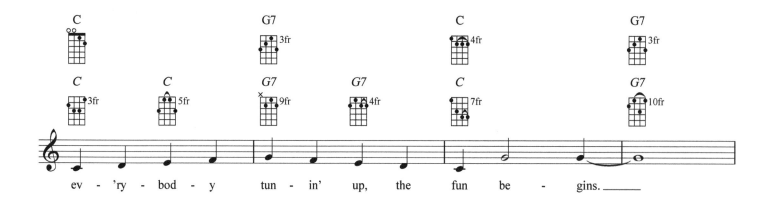

ev - 'ry - bod - y tun - in' up, the fun be - gins. _____

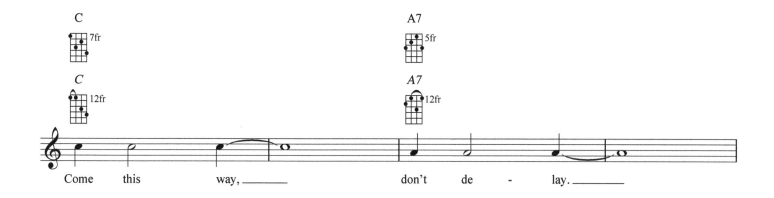

Come this way, _____ don't de - lay. _____

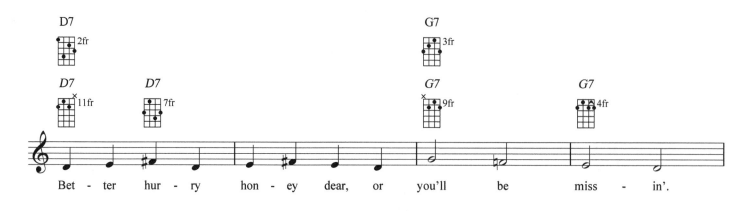

Bet - ter hur - ry hon - ey dear, or you'll be miss - in'.

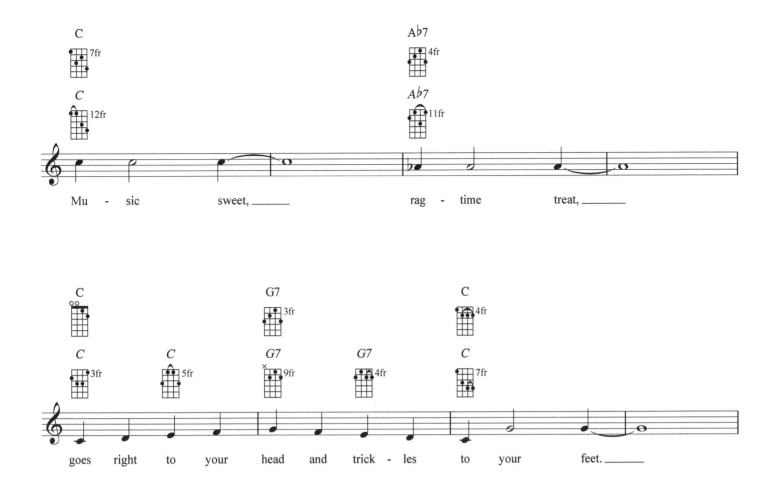

Mu - sic sweet, _____ rag - time treat, _____

goes right to your head and trick - les to your feet. _____

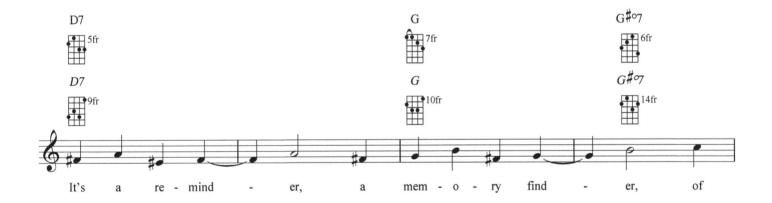

It's a re - mind - er, a mem - o - ry find - er, of

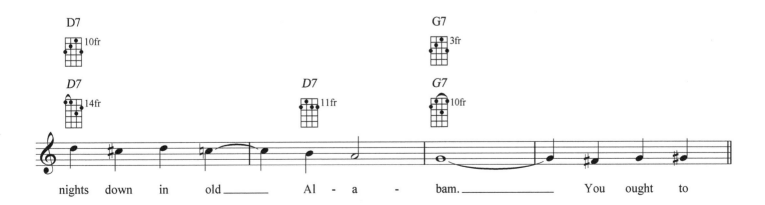

nights down in old _____ Al - a - bam. _____ You ought to

Chorus

see Dea - con Jones _____ when he rat - tles them bones, _____

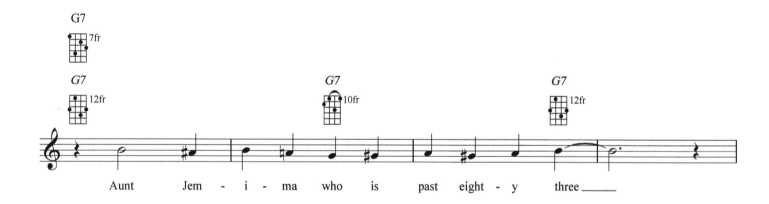

Old Par - son Brown _____ danc - in' 'round like a clown, _____

Aunt Jem - i - ma who is past eight - y three _____

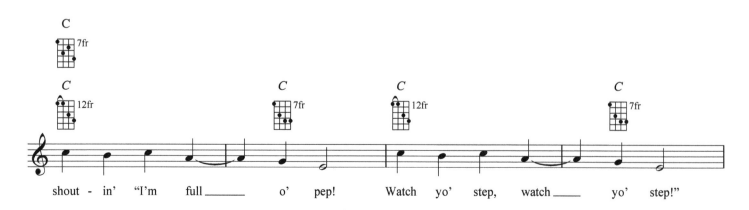

shout - in' "I'm full _____ o' pep! Watch yo' step, watch _____ yo' step!"

Alabamy Bound

from THE GREAT AMERICAN BROADCAST
Words by B.G. DeSylva and Bud Green
Music by Ray Henderson

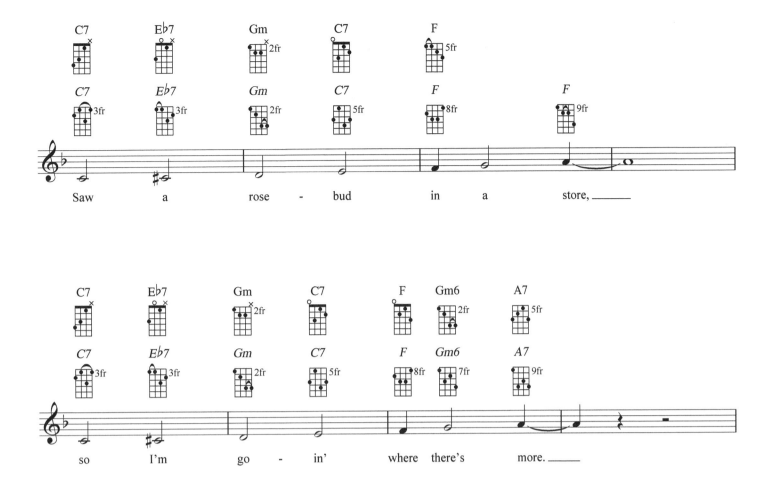

Saw a rose - bud in a store, _____ so I'm go - in' where there's more. _____

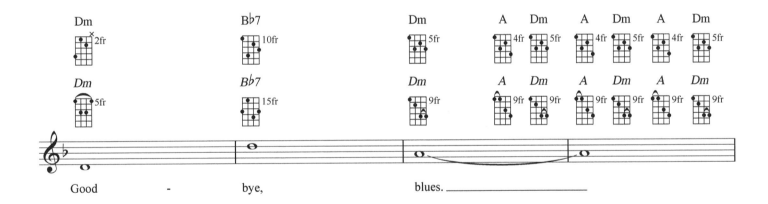

Good - bye, blues. _____

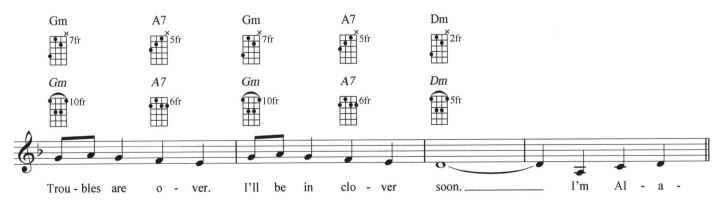

Trou - bles are o - ver. I'll be in clo - ver soon. _____ I'm Al - a -

Chorus

bam - y   bound. _____   There'll   be   no   "hee - bie   jee - bies"

hang - in'   'round. _____   Just   gave   the   mean - est   tick - et

man   on   earth _____   all   I'm   worth _____

to   put   my   toot - sies   in   an   up - per   berth. _____   { Just   hear   that
                                                                { I'm   just   a

Alexander's Ragtime Band

from ALEXANDER'S RAGTIME BAND
Words and Music by Irving Berlin

Verse
Medium bright

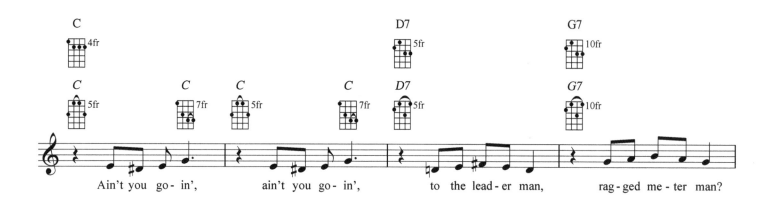

Oh, ma hon-ey, oh, ma hon-ey, bet-ter hur-ry and let's me-an-der.

Ain't you go-in', ain't you go-in', to the lead-er man, rag-ged me-ter man?

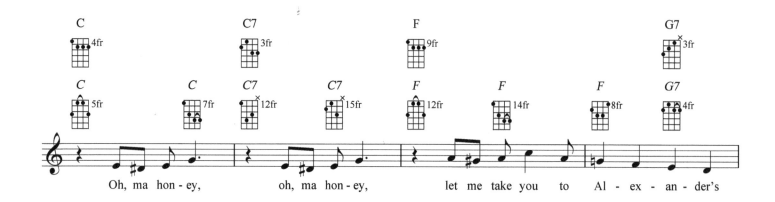

Oh, ma hon-ey, oh, ma hon-ey, let me take you to Al-ex-an-der's

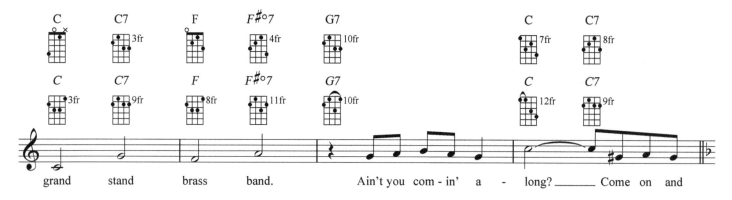

grand stand brass band. Ain't you com-in' a - long? _____ Come on and

Chorus

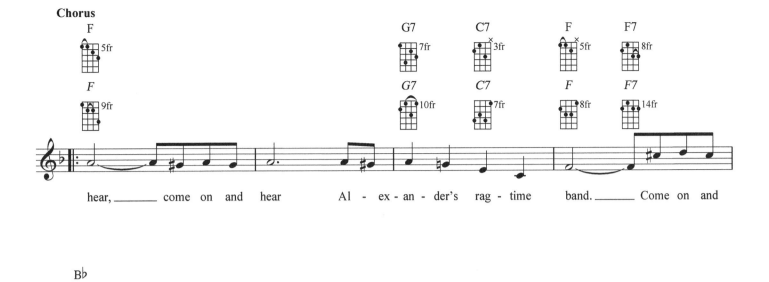

hear, _____ come on and hear Al - ex - an - der's rag - time band. _____ Come on and

hear, _____ come on and hear. It's the best band in the land. They can

play a bu - gle call like you nev - er heard be - fore, so nat - ur - al that you want to go to war.

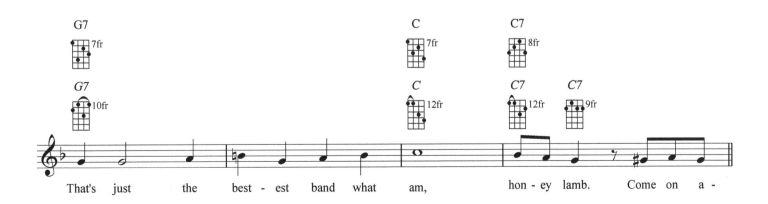

That's just the best - est band what am, hon - ey lamb. Come on a -

long, _____ come on a - long, let me take you by the hand _____ up to the

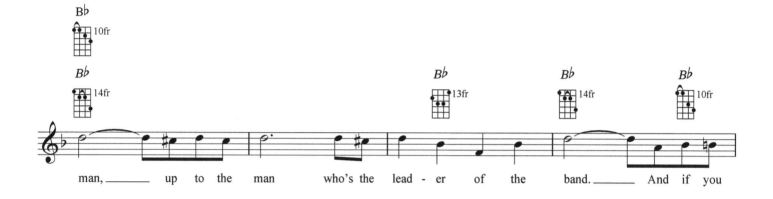

man, _____ up to the man who's the lead - er of the band. _____ And if you

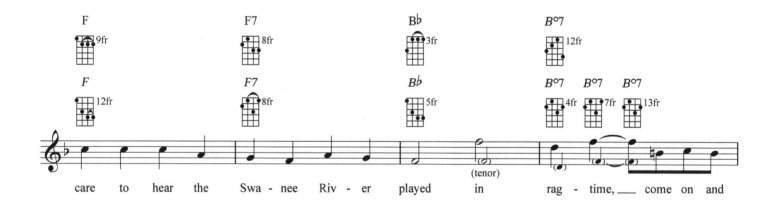

care to hear the Swa - nee Riv - er played in rag - time, ___ come on and

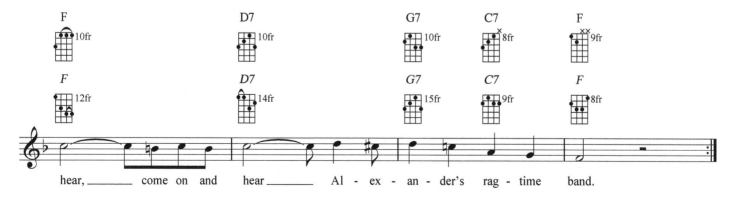

hear, _____ come on and hear _____ Al - ex - an - der's rag - time band.

Breezin' Along with the Breeze

Words by Haven Gillespie and Seymour Simons
Music by Richard A. Whiting

Chorus

I'm just breez-in' a - long __ with the breeze, _____ trail-in' the

rails, _____ roam - in' the seas.

Like the bird - ies that sing __ in the trees, _____ pleas - in' to

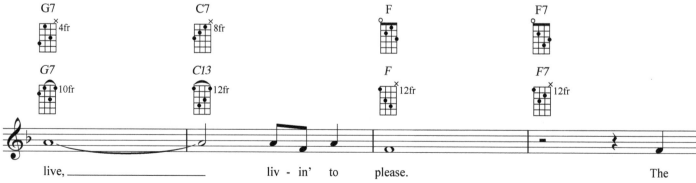

live, _____ liv - in' to please. The

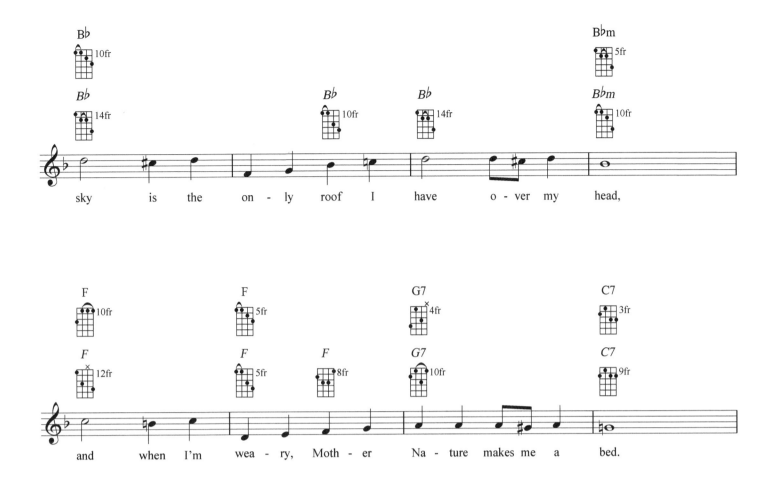

sky   is   the   on - ly   roof   I   have   o - ver my   head,

and   when   I'm   wea - ry,   Moth - er   Na - ture makes me a   bed.

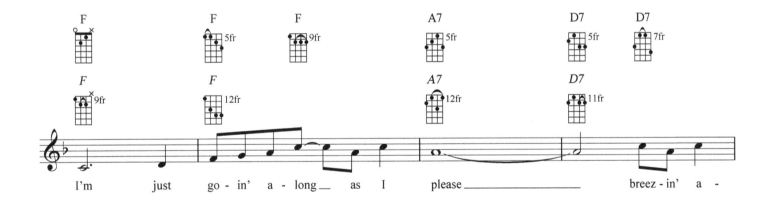

I'm   just   go - in' a - long as I   please   breez - in' a -

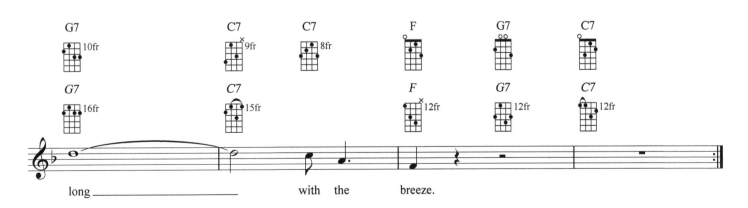

long   with the   breeze.

At Sundown

Words and Music by Walter Donaldson

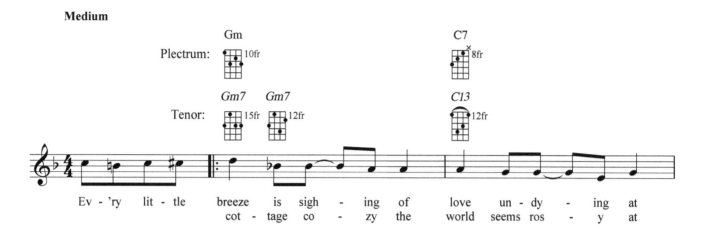

Ev - 'ry lit - tle breeze is sigh - ing of love un - dy - ing at
cot - tage co - zy the world seems ros - y at

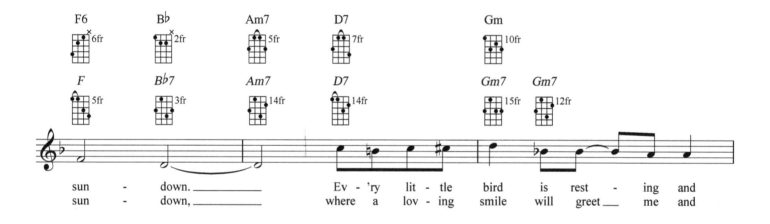

sun - down. _____ Ev - 'ry lit - tle bird is rest - ing and
sun - down, _____ where a lov - ing smile will greet ___ me and

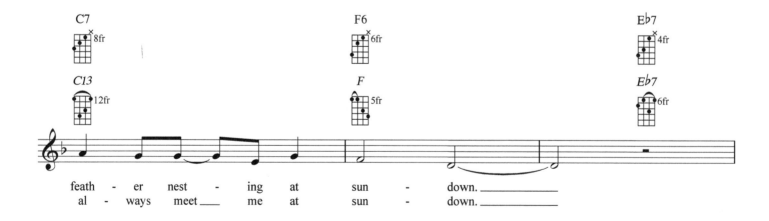

feath - er nest - ing at sun - down. _____
al - ways meet ___ me at sun - down. _____

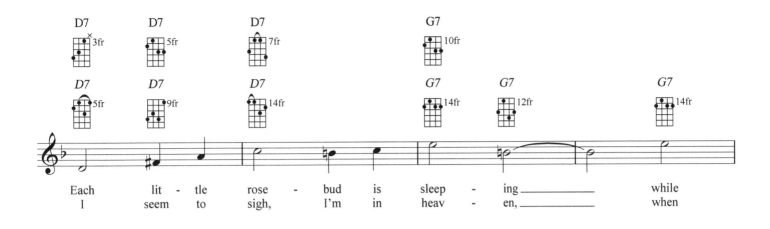

Each little rose - bud is sleep - ing _____ while
I seem to sigh, I'm in heav - en, _____ when

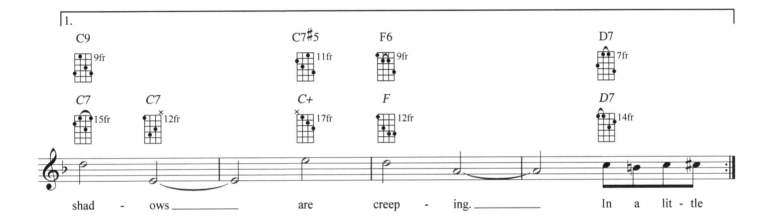

shad - ows _____ are creep - ing. _____ In a lit - tle

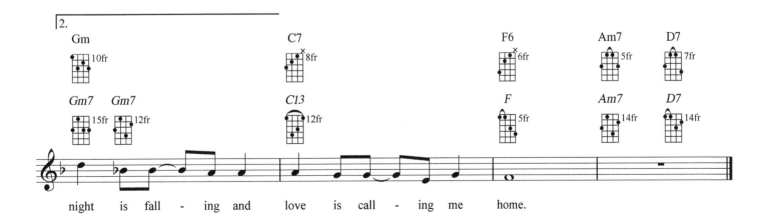

night is fall - ing and love is call - ing me home.

Avalon

Words by Al Jolson and B.G. DeSylva
Music by Vincent Rose

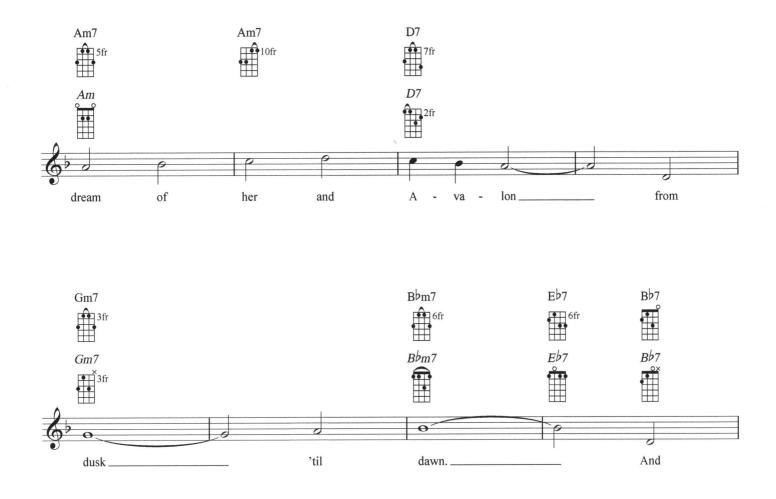

dream   of   her   and   A - va - lon _____ from

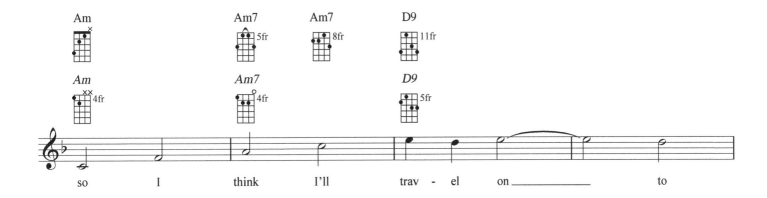

dusk _____ 'til   dawn. _____ And

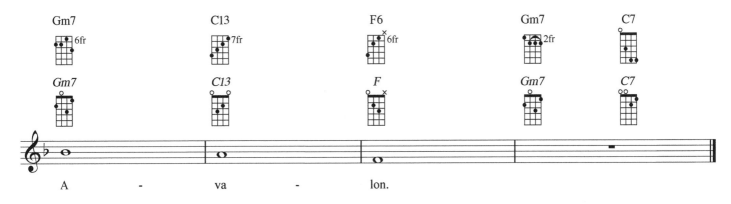

so   I   think   I'll   trav - el   on _____ to

Gm7   C13   F6   Gm7   C7

Gm7   C13   F   Gm7   C7

A -   va -   lon.

Baby Face

Words and Music by Benny Davis and Harry Akst

want to live with - out her; I love her good - ness knows. I
win - nin' ev - 'ry rib - bon with your sweet ba - by way. Say,

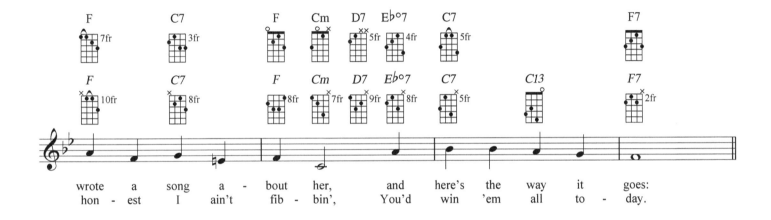

wrote a song a - bout her, and here's the way it goes:
hon - est I ain't fib - bin', You'd win 'em all to - day.

Chorus
Medium fast

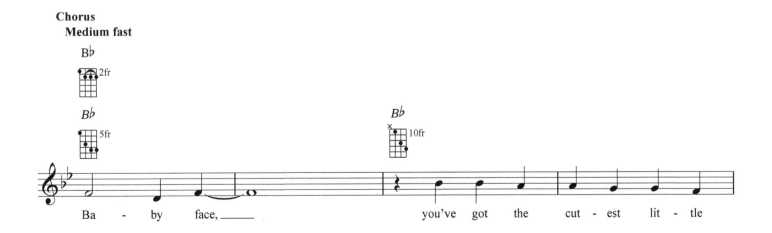

Ba - by face, _____ you've got the cut - est lit - tle

ba - by face. _____ There's not an - oth - er one could

take your place, _____ ba - by face. _____

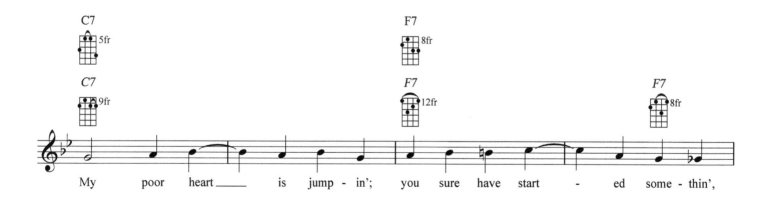

My poor heart _____ is jump - in'; you sure have start - ed some - thin',

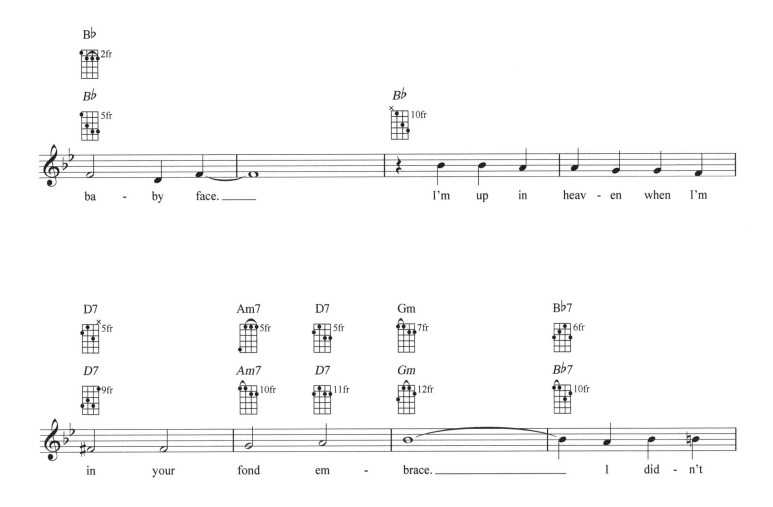

ba - by face. _____ I'm up in heav - en when I'm

in your fond em - brace. _____ I did - n't

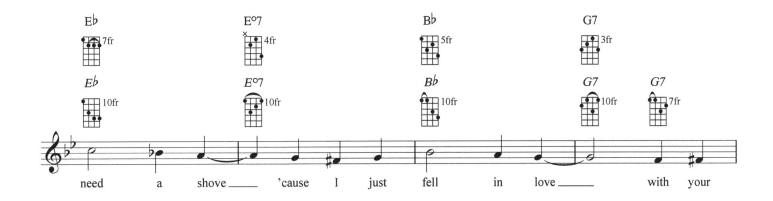

need a shove _____ 'cause I just fell in love _____ with your

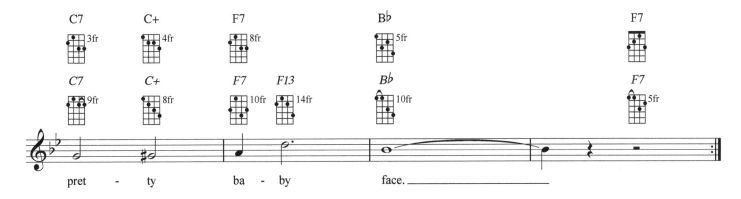

pret - ty ba - by face. _____

Basin Street Blues

Words and Music by Spencer Williams

Verse
Medium slow

Won't-cha come a-long with me, 'long the Mis-sis-sip-pi?

We'll take a boat to the land of dreams, _ steam down the riv-er down to New Or-leans. _ A

band there to meet us, old friends to greet us,

you'll see the place where the folks all meet. _ Heav-en on earth they call it Ba-sin Street. _

Chorus

Ba - sin Street is the street __ where all good friends __ al - ways meet __ in

New Or - leans, __ land of dreams. __ You'll nev - er know how nice it seems or just how much it real - ly means.

Glad to be, __ yes sir - ree, __ where her wel - come streets __ wel - come me. __ Where

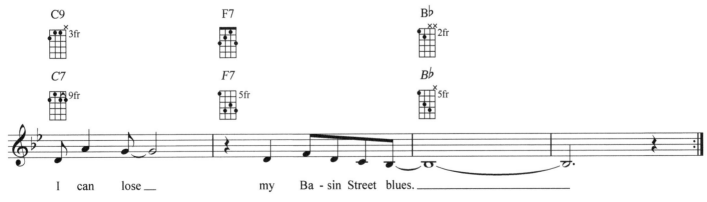

I can lose __ my Ba - sin Street blues. _____

Bei Mir Bist Du Schon
(Means That You're Grand)

Original Words by Jacob Jacobs
Music by Sholom Secunda
English Version by Sammy Cahn and Saul Chaplin

Verse
Medium Swing

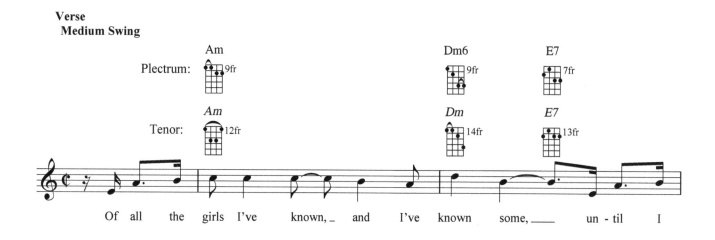

Of all the girls I've known, ___ and I've known some, ___ un - til I

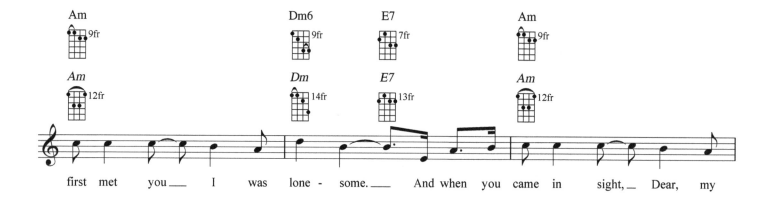

first met you ___ I was lone - some. ___ And when you came in sight, ___ Dear, my

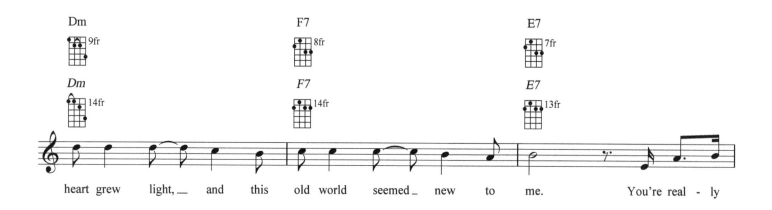

heart grew light, ___ and this old world seemed ___ new to me. You're real - ly

swell I have to ad - mit. You ___ de - serve ex - press - sions that ___ real - ly

fit you. ___ And so I've racked my brain, ___ hop - ing to ex - plain ___ all the

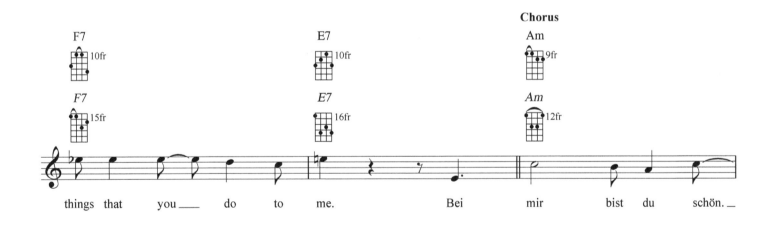

Chorus

things that you ___ do to me. Bei mir bist du schön. ___

___ Please let me ex - plain. ___ Bei

mir   bist   du   schön _____ means   that _____ you're   grand. _____

Bei   mir   bist   du   schön. _____   A -

gain   I'll   ex - plain. _____   (Boy) It   means   you're   the   fair -
                                                          (Girl) It   means   that   my   heart's

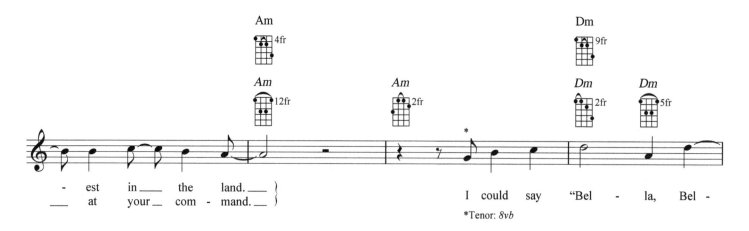

- est   in _____ the   land. _____   }
_____ at   your _ com - mand. _____ }
                                                                     I   could   say   "Bel - la,   Bel -

*Tenor: *8vb*

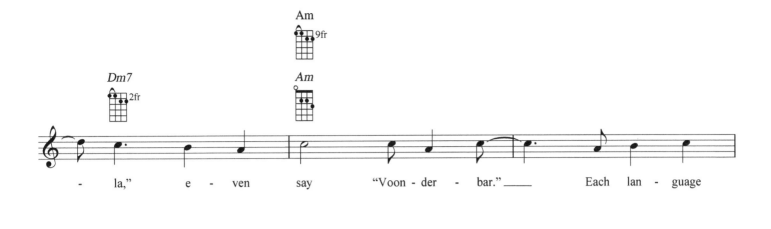

-la," e - ven say "Voon - der - bar." ____ Each lan - guage

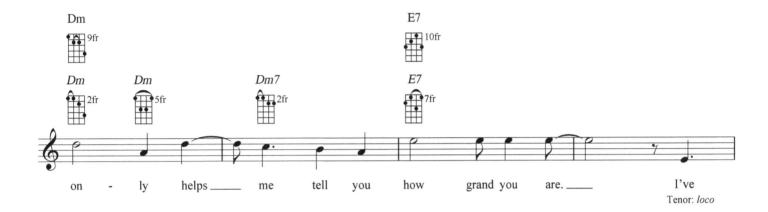

on - ly helps ____ me tell you how grand you are. ____ I've

Tenor: *loco*

tried to ex - plain, ___ Bei mir bist du schön, ___ so

kiss me and say ____ you un - der - stand. ___

Bill Bailey,
Won't You Please Come Home

Words and Music by Hughie Cannon

Verse
Medium Bright

1. On one sum - mer day, _____ the sun was shin - in' fine, _
2. Bill drove by that door, _____ in an aut - 'mo - bile, _

the la - dy hon - ey of old Bill Bail - ey she
a great big di - a - mond, coach and foot - man to

hung clothes on the line _____ in her back yard _____
hear that big wench squeal. _____ "He's all a - lone," _____

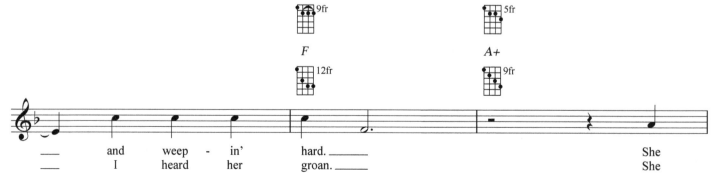

_____ and weep - in' hard. _____ She
_____ I heard her groan. _____ She

Chorus

"Won't you come home, Bill Bail - ley, won't you come home?"

She moans the whole day long. _____

"I'll do the cook - in', dar - lin'. I'll pay the rent.

I know I've done you wrong. _____

Blue Skies

from BETSY
Words and Music by Irving Berlin

Bye Bye Blackbird

from PETE KELLY'S BLUES

Lyric by Mort Dixon
Music by Ray Henderson

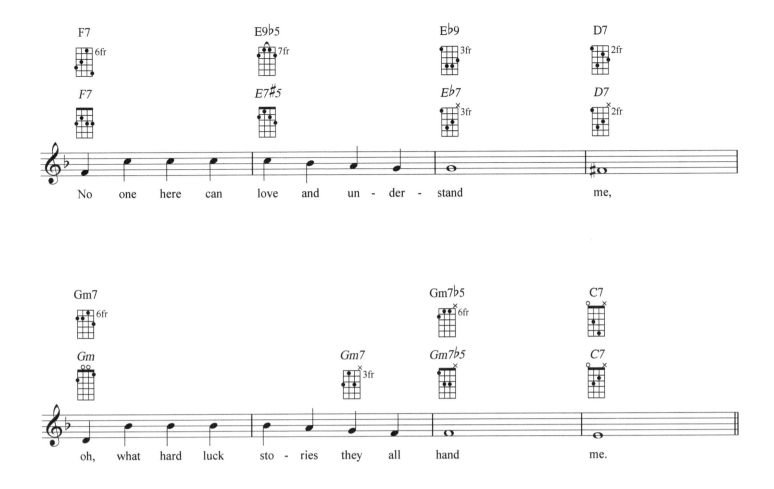

No one here can love and un - der - stand me,

me,

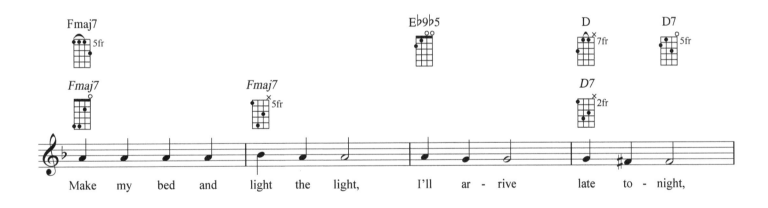

oh, what hard luck sto - ries they all hand me.

Make my bed and light the light, I'll ar - rive late to - night,

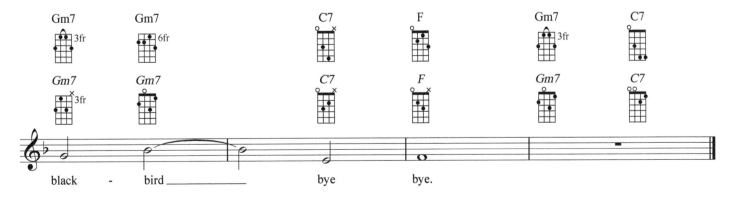

black - bird _____ bye bye.

Bye Bye Blues

Words and Music by Fred Hamm, Dave Bennett, Bert Lown and Chauncey Gray

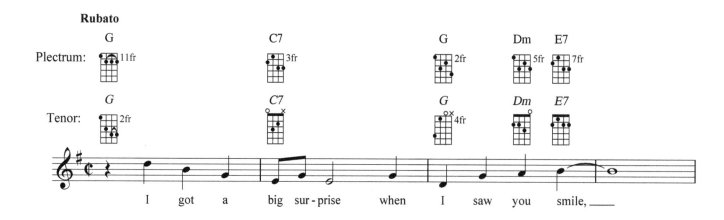

I got a big sur-prise when I saw you smile, ____

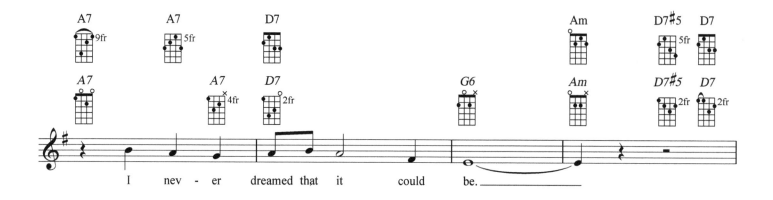

I nev - er dreamed that it could be. _____

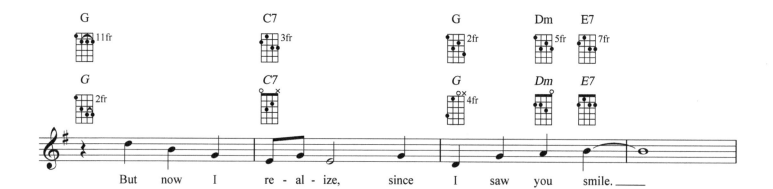

But now I re - al - ize, since I saw you smile. ____

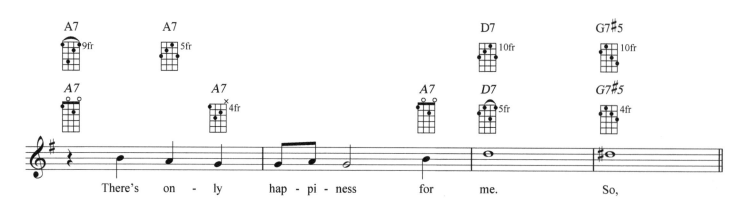

There's on - ly hap - pi - ness for me. So,

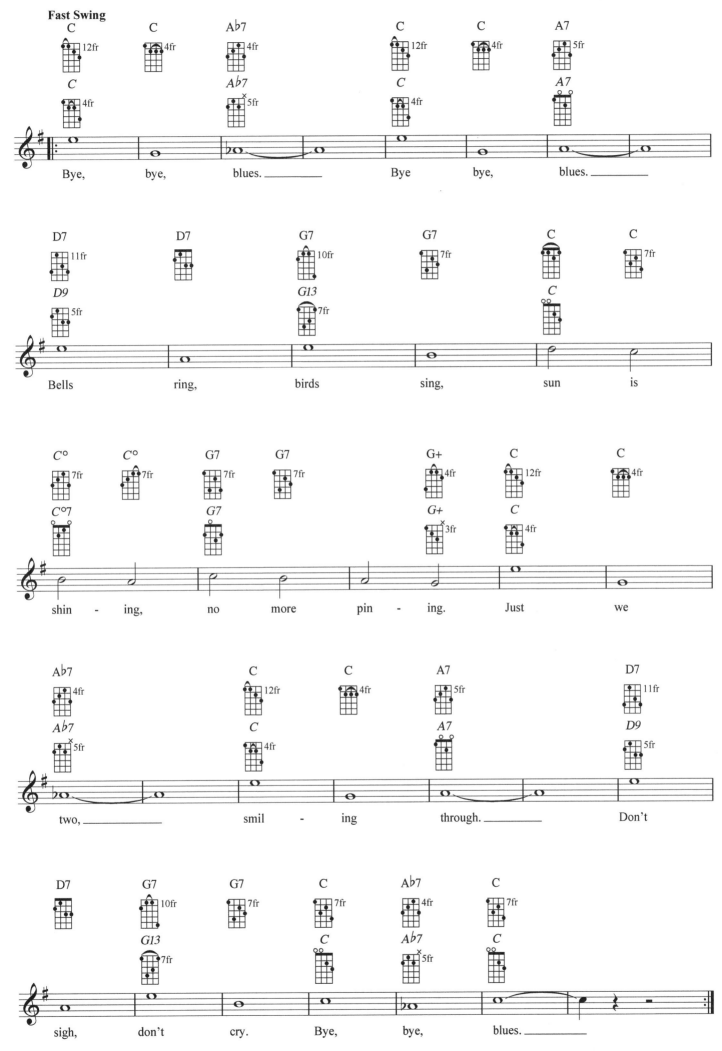

Fast Swing

Bye, bye, blues. _____ Bye bye, blues. _____

Bells ring, birds sing, sun is

shin - ing, no more pin - ing. Just we

two, _____ smil - ing through. _____ Don't

sigh, don't cry. Bye, bye, blues. _____

California, Here I Come

Words and Music by Al Jolson, B.G. DeSylva and Joseph Meyer

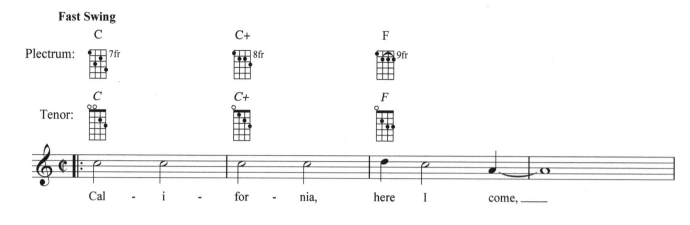

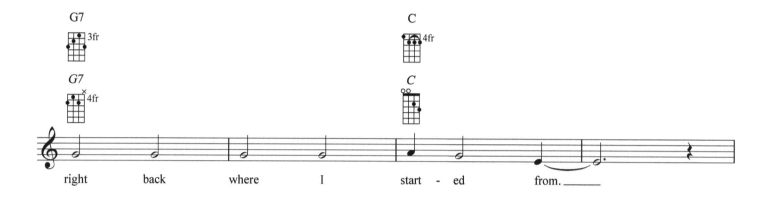

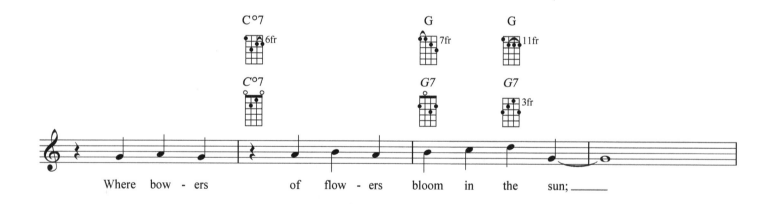

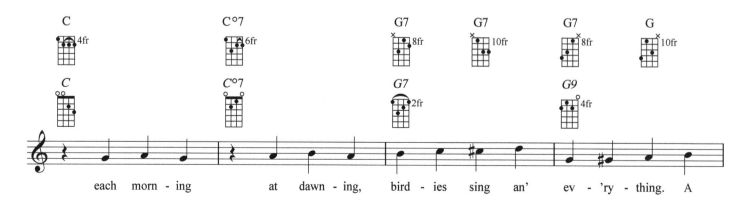

sun - kissed   miss   said,   "Don't   be   late." _____

That's   why   I   can   hard - ly   wait. _____

O - pen   up   that   Gold - en   Gate; _____   Cal - i -

for - nia,   here   I   come! _____

Chinatown, My Chinatown

Words by William Jerome
Music by Jean Schwartz

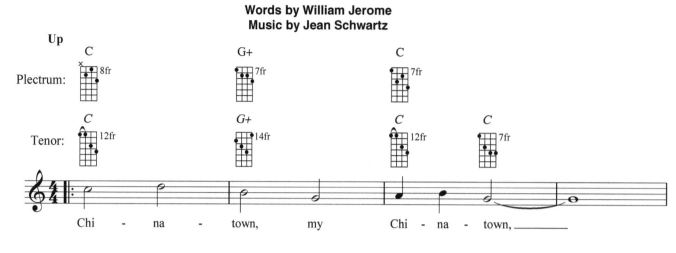

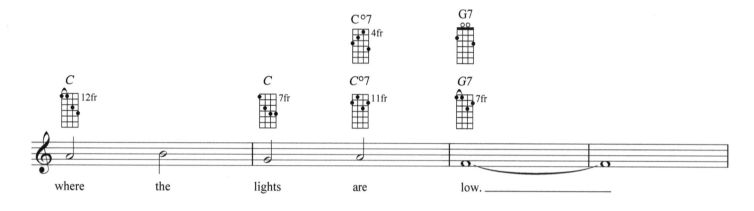

where the lights are low. _____

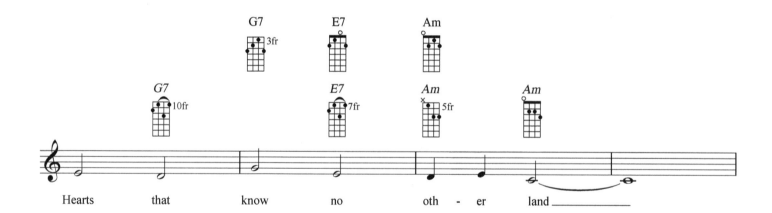

Hearts that know no oth-er land _____

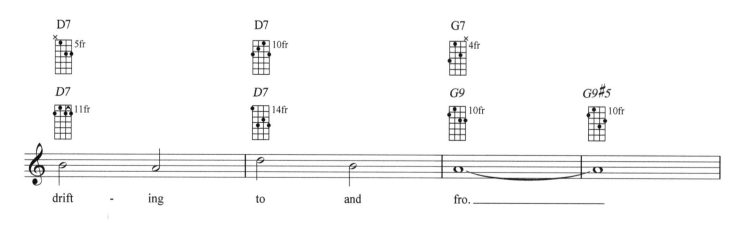

drift-ing to and fro. _____

'Deed I Do

Words and Music by Walter Hirsch and Fred Rose

Chorus
Bright

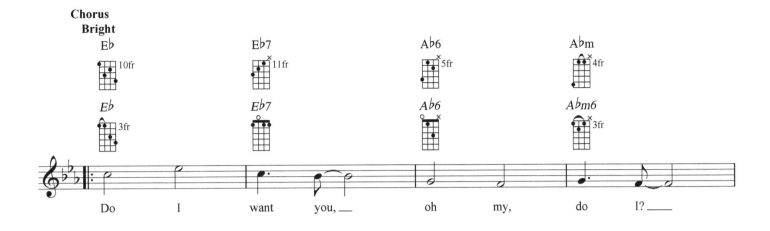

Do I want you, ___ oh my, do I? ___

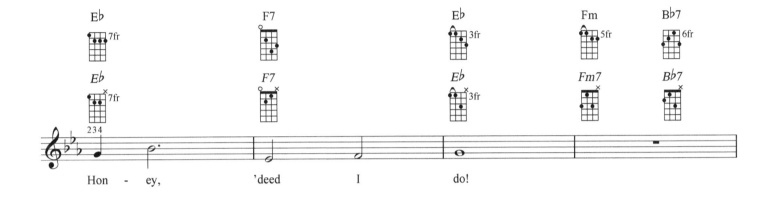

Hon - ey, 'deed I do!

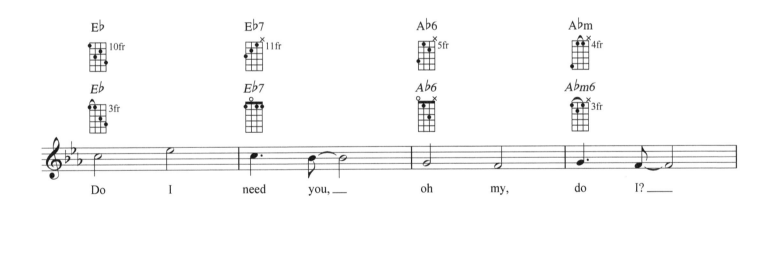

Do I need you, ___ oh my, do I? ___

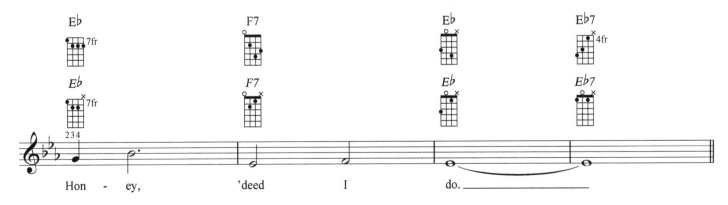

Hon - ey, 'deed I do. _____

Bridge

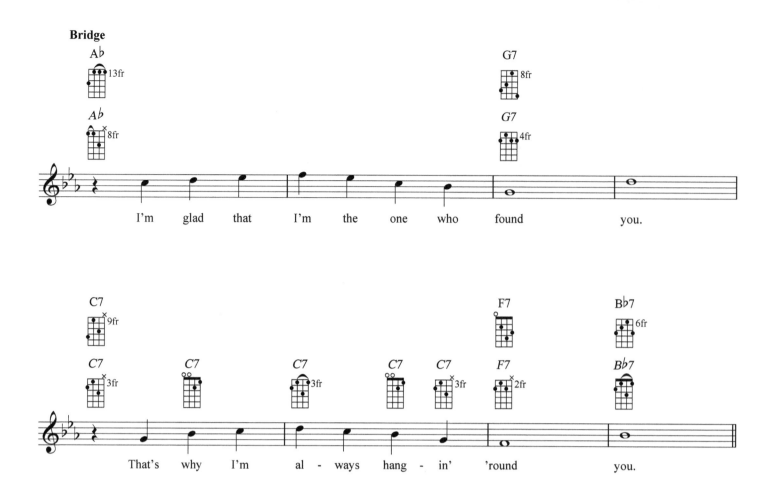

I'm glad that I'm the one who found you.

That's why I'm al - ways hang - in' 'round you.

Chorus

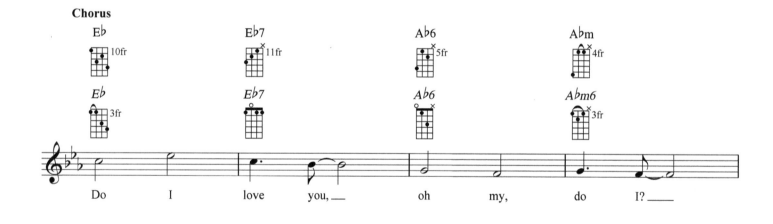

Do I love you, ___ oh my, do I? ___

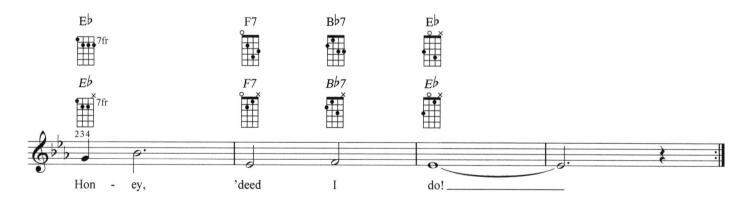

Hon - ey, 'deed I do! _____

Dinah

from THE BIG BROADCAST
Words by Sam M. Lewis and Joe Young
Music by Harry Akst

Verse
Rubato

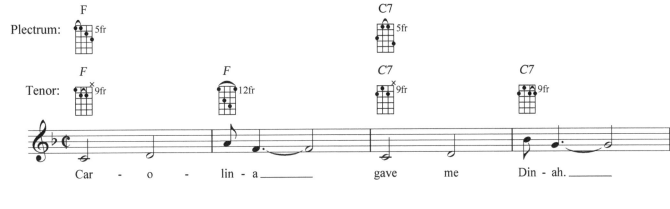

Car - o - lin - a _____ gave me Din - ah. _____

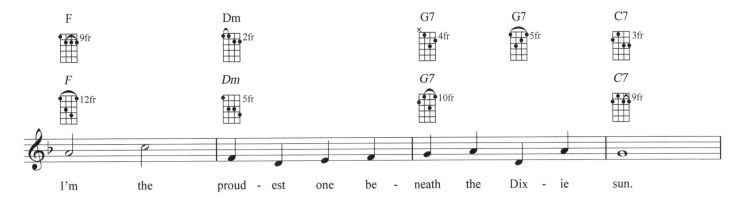

I'm the proud - est one be - neath the Dix - ie sun.

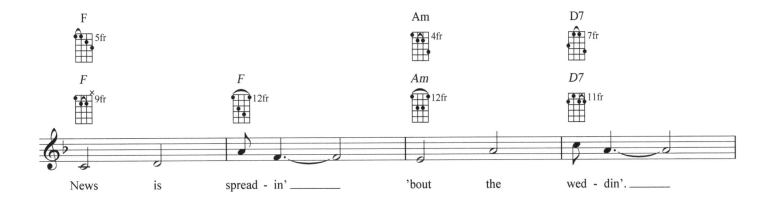

News is spread - in' _____ 'bout the wed - din'. _____

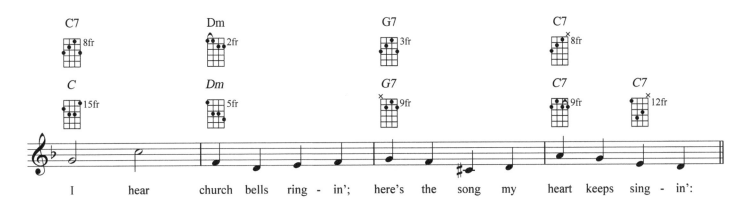

I hear church bells ring - in'; here's the song my heart keeps sing - in':

Chorus

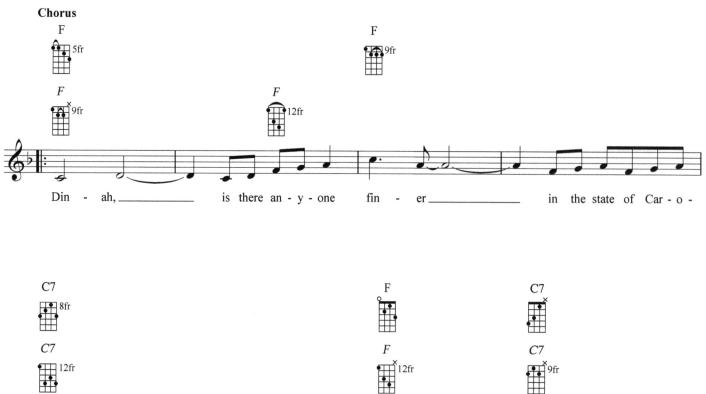

Din - ah,_____ is there an - y - one fin - er_____ in the state of Car - o -

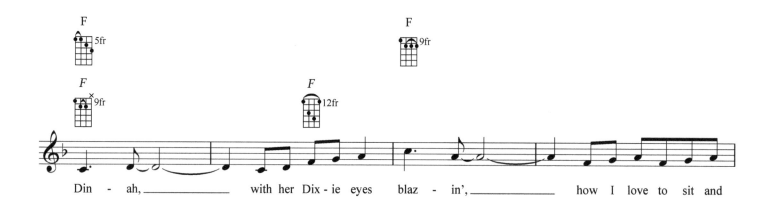

lin - a?_____ If there is and you know her, __ show 'er to me. __

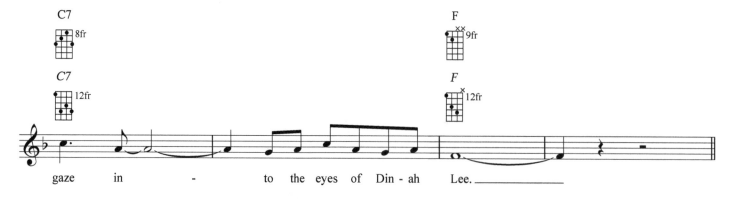

Din - ah,_____ with her Dix - ie eyes blaz - in',_____ how I love to sit and

gaze in - to the eyes of Din - ah Lee._____

Bridge

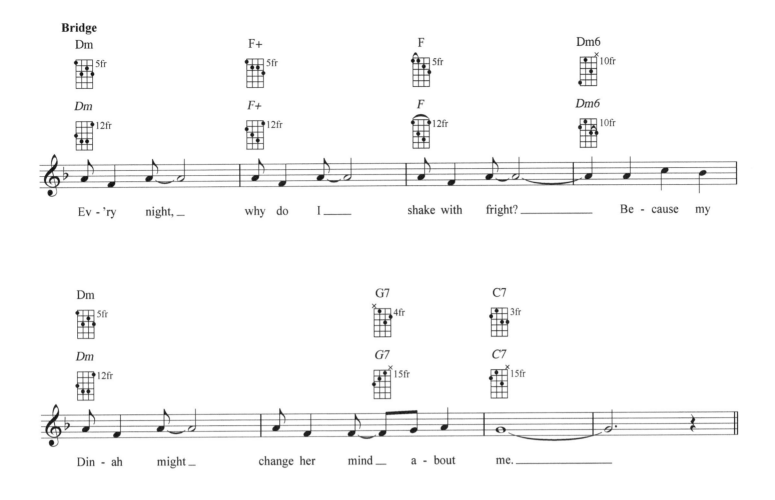

Ev-'ry night,__ why do I ____ shake with fright? _____ Be - cause my

Din - ah might __ change her mind __ a - bout me. _____

Chorus

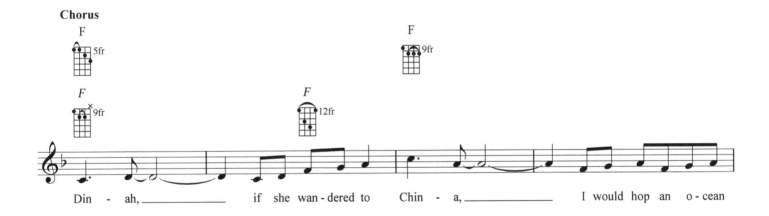

Din - ah, _____ if she wan - dered to Chin - a, _____ I would hop an o - cean

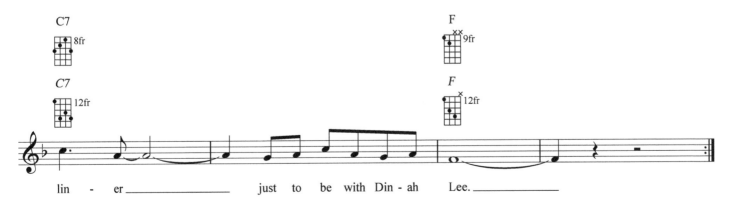

lin - er _____ just to be with Din - ah Lee. _____

Do You Know What It Means to Miss New Orleans

Written by Eddie De Lange and Louis Alter

dream _____ a-bout mag - nol - ias in June, _ and soon I'm wish-in' that I _____ was there. _ Do you

know what it means _ to miss New Or - leans _ when that's where you left _ your

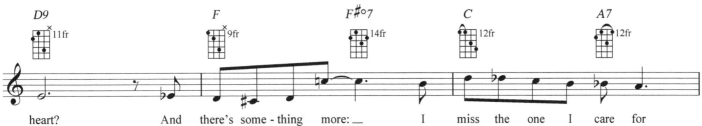

heart? And there's some - thing more: _ I miss the one I care for

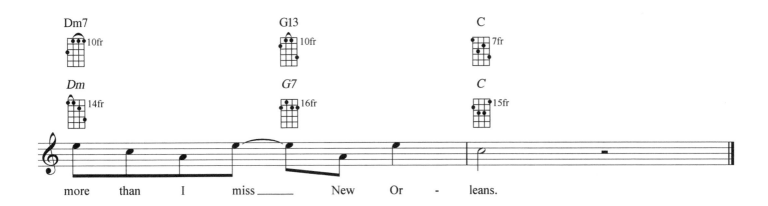

more than I miss _____ New Or - leans.

Georgia on My Mind

Words by Stuart Gorrell
Music by Hoagy Carmichael

Honeysuckle Rose

from AIN'T MISBEHAVIN'
Words by Andy Razaf
Music by Thomas "Fats" Waller

Medium

Ev - 'ry hon - ey bee
When you're pass - in' by,

fills with jeal - ous - y
flow - ers droop and sigh,

when they see you out with
and I know the rea - son

me.   I don't blame them, }
why: you're much sweet - er, }

good - ness knows, _____

hon - ey - suck - le rose. _____

_____ rose. _____

Don't   buy   sug - ar;

you just ___ have to touch my cup. ___ You're my sug - ar;

it's sweet ___ when you stir it up. ___ When I'm tak - in' sips

from your tas - ty lips, seems the hon - ey fair - ly drips. You're con - fec - tion,

good - ness knows, _____ hon - ey - suck - le rose. _____

I Got Rhythm

from AN AMERICAN IN PARIS
Music and Lyrics by George Gershwin and Ira Gershwin

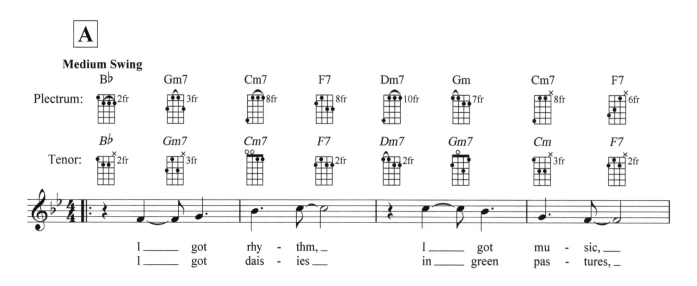

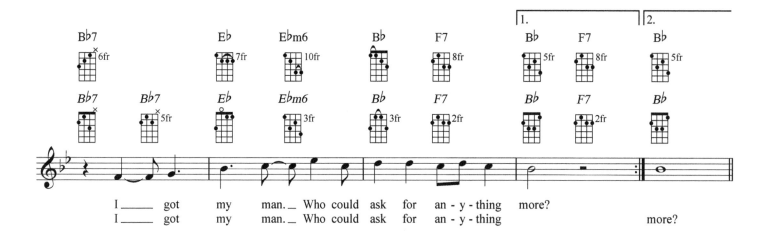

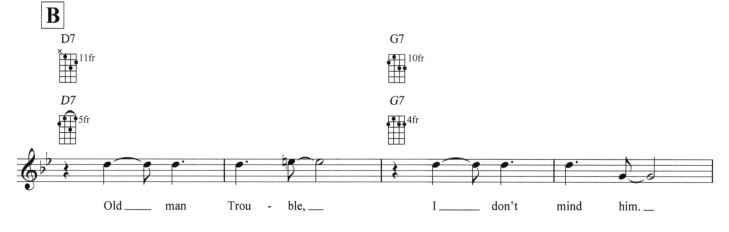

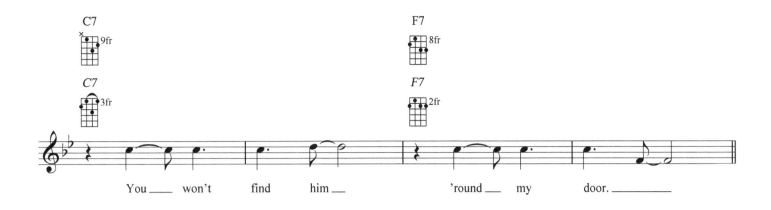

You ___ won't find him ___ 'round ___ my door. ___

A

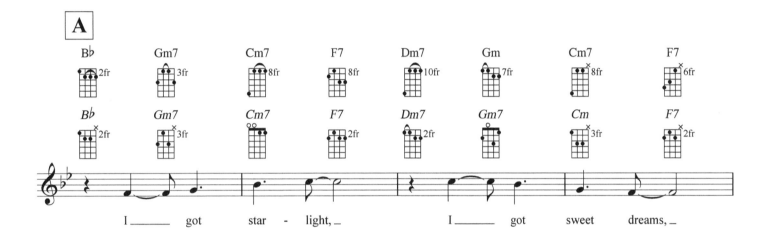

I _____ got star - light, ___ I _____ got sweet dreams, ___

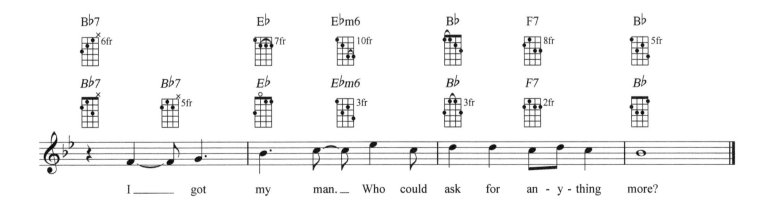

I _____ got my man. ___ Who could ask for an - y - thing more?

65

In a Shanty in Old Shanty Town

Lyric by Joe Young
Music by Jack Little and Ira Schuster

Chorus

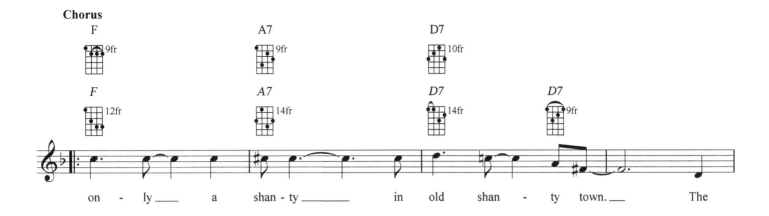

on - ly ___ a shan - ty ___ in old shan - ty town. ___ The

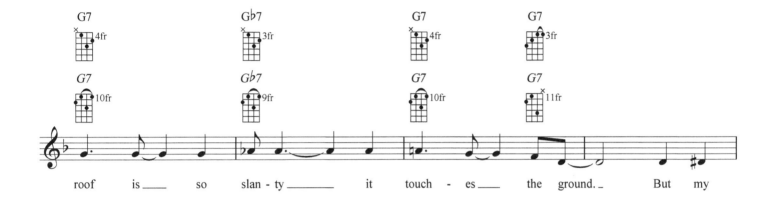

roof is ___ so slan - ty ___ it touch - es ___ the ground. ___ But my

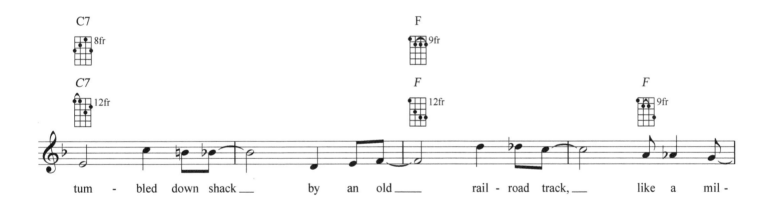

tum - bled down shack ___ by an old ___ rail - road track, ___ like a mil -

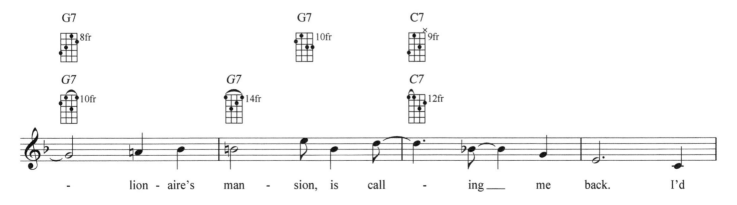

- lion - aire's man - sion, is call - ing ___ me back. I'd

give up ___ a pal - ace _____ if I were ___ a king. ___ It's

more than ___ a pal - ace; _____ it's my ev - 'ry - thing. ___ There's a

queen wait - ing there with a sil - ver - y crown ___ in a

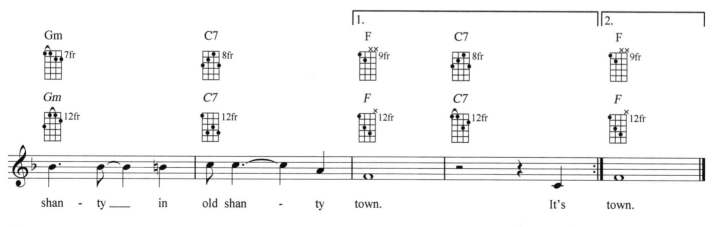

shan - ty ___ in old shan - ty town. It's town.

Ja-Da

Words and Music by Bob Carleton

ain't much to the words but the mu - sic is grand, ___ and
ob - ject ___ now ___ is for some - thing new, ___

you'll be sing - ing it to beat ___ the band. ___ Now you've heard of you "Will
some - thing that will ap - peal ___ to you. ___ And here's little mel - o - dy

o' ___ the Wisp," ___ but give a lit - tle lis - ten to this; ___ it goes:
that you will find, ___ will ling - er, ling - er there in your mind; ___ it goes:

Chorus

Ja - da, Ja - da, Ja - da Ja - da Jing, Jing, Jing.

Ja - da,   Ja - da,   Ja - da Ja - da Jing, Jing,   Jing.

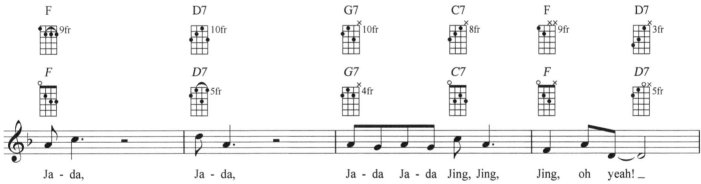

That's a fun-ny lit-tle bit of mel - o - dy; __ it's so sooth-ing and ap-peal-ing to me. __ It goes

Ja - da,   Ja - da,   Ja - da Ja - da Jing, Jing,   Jing, oh yeah! __

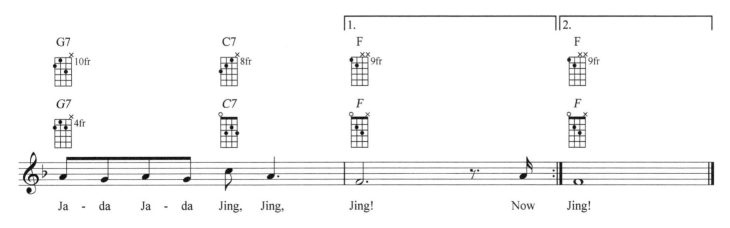

Ja - da Ja - da Jing, Jing,   Jing!   Now Jing!

The Jazz-Me Blues

Words and Music by Tom Delaney

1. Down in Lou - si - an - a in that sun - ny clime, ___ they
2. Ev - 'ry - bod - y now a days ___ does that dance. ___ You'd

play a class of mu - sic that is sup - er fine. ___ And it
bet - ter learn to jazz now while you've got the chance. ___ This

make no dif - fer - ence if it's ___ rain or shine, ___ you can
pleas - ing synch - o - pa - tion has ___ come to stay. ___ Now ___

hear that jazz - in' mu - sic play - ing all the time. ___ It
all you've got to do is just to jazz a - way. ___ So

sounds so pe - cu - li - ar 'cause the mu - sic's queer, ___
when you hear that band ___ play - ing at the ball, ___

how its sweet vi - bra - tion seems to fill the air ___
grab your gal and do your stuff a - round the hall. ___ With ___

Then to you the whole world seems to be in rhyme, ___ you want
noth - ing on your mind but mu - sic and your brown, ___ on - ly

Break -

noth - ing else but jazz - in', jazz - in' all the time. ___
wait - ing for the time so you can jazz her 'round. ___

Ev - 'ry - one _____ that's night nev - er seems ___ to sigh,
Take your time _____ and sway, throw your - self _____ a - way.

hear them loud - ly cry: Oh! } Jazz me, _____
Let me hear you say: Oh! }

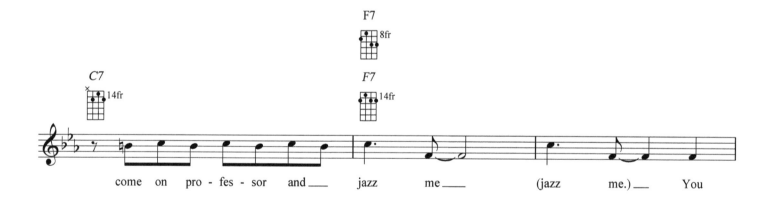

come on pro - fes - sor and ___ jazz me _____ (jazz me.) ___ You

know I like my danc - in' both ___ day and night, ___ and if I don't get my jazz - in', I

Lazy River

from THE BEST YEARS OF OUR LIVES
Words and Music by Hoagy Carmichael and Sidney Arodin

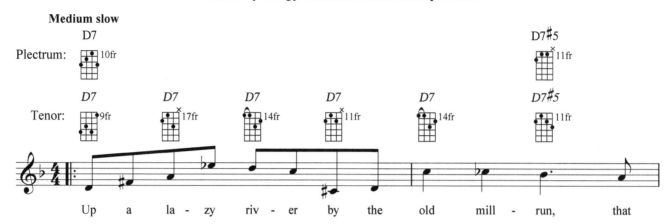

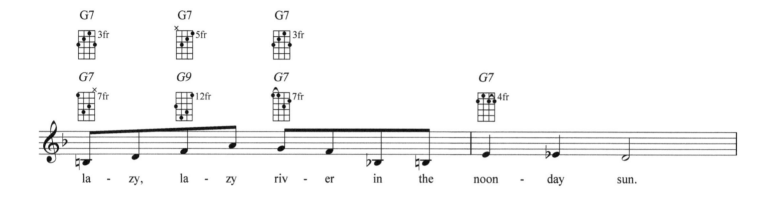

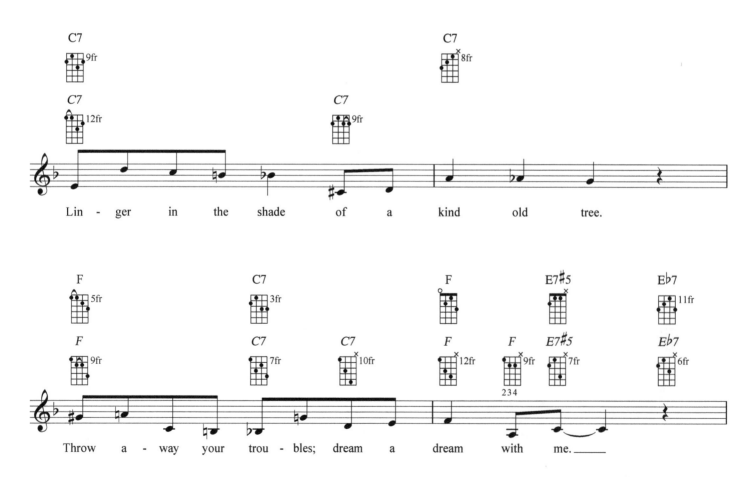

Mississippi Mud

Words and Music by James Cavanaugh and Harry Barris

B

What a dance __ do they do! __ Lord - y, how I'm tell - in' you. __

They don't need no band; they keep time by clap - pin' their hand. Just as

hap - py as a cow chew - in' on a cud, when the

Fine

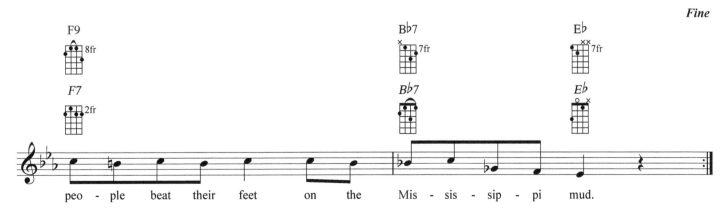

peo - ple beat their feet on the Mis - sis - sip - pi mud.

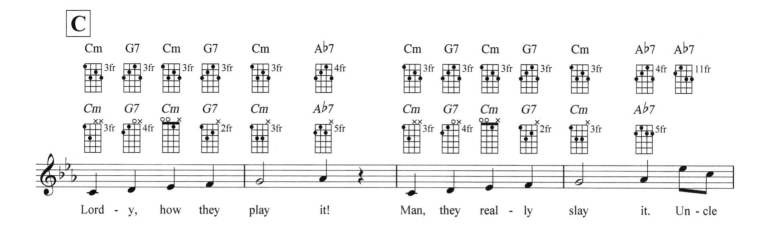

Lord - y, how they play it! Man, they real - ly slay it. Un - cle

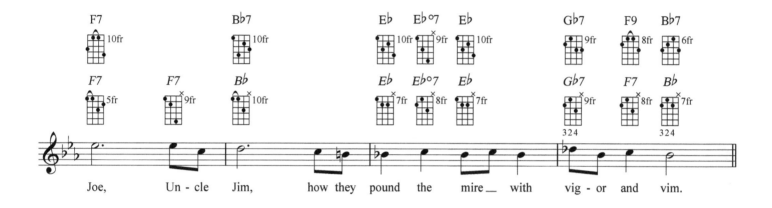

Joe, Un - cle Jim, how they pound the mire __ with vig - or and vim.

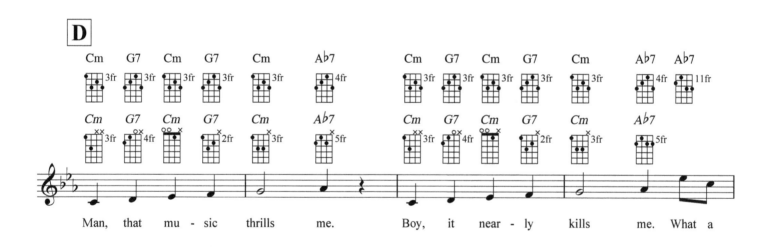

Man, that mu - sic thrills me. Boy, it near - ly kills me. What a

D.S. al Fine

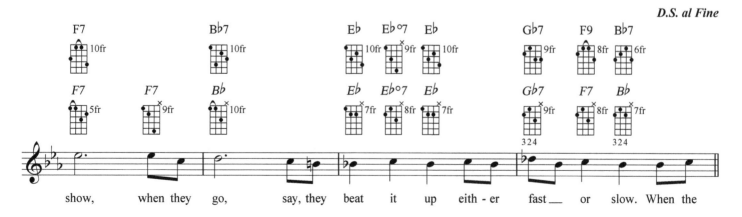

show, when they go, say, they beat it up eith - er fast __ or slow. When the

My Honey's Loving Arms

Words by Herman Ruby
Music by Joseph Meyer

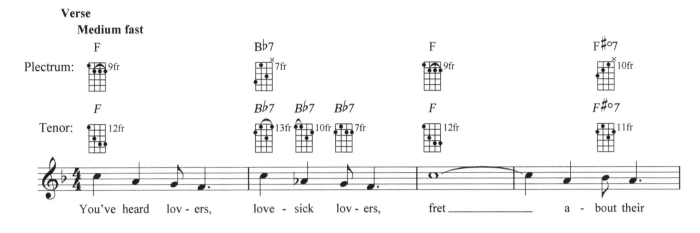

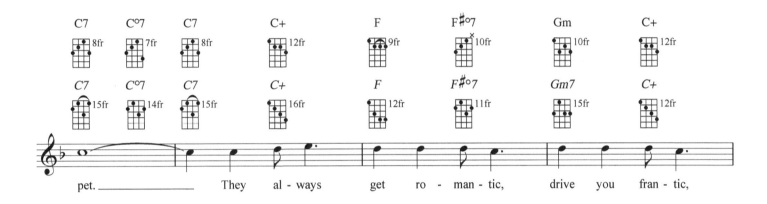

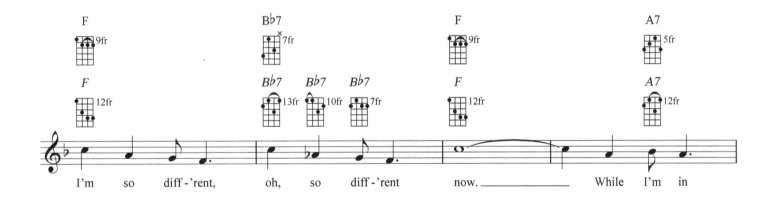

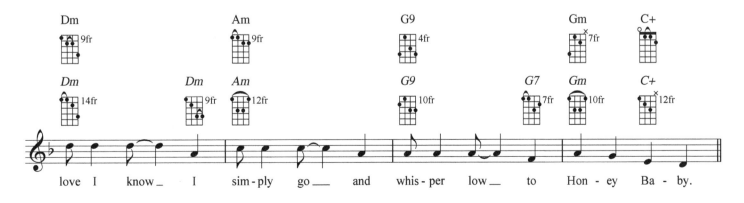

Chorus

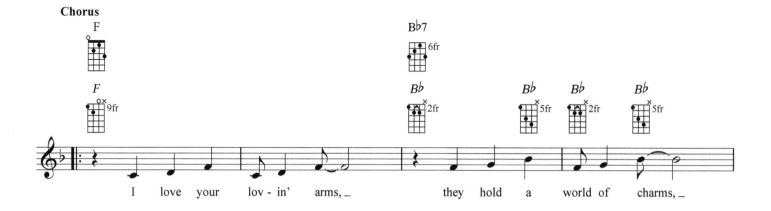

I love your lov - in' arms, _ they hold a world of charms, _

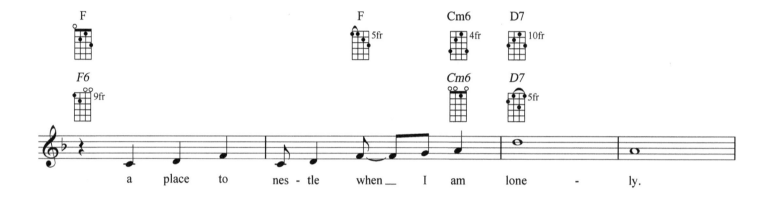

a place to nes - tle when _ I am lone - ly.

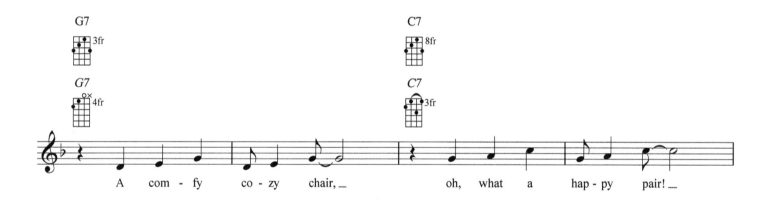

A com - fy co - zy chair, _ oh, what a hap - py pair! _

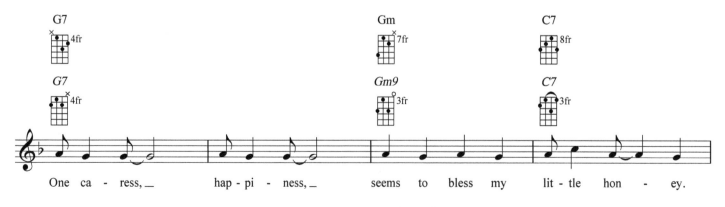

One ca - ress, _ hap - pi - ness, _ seems to bless my lit - tle hon - ey.

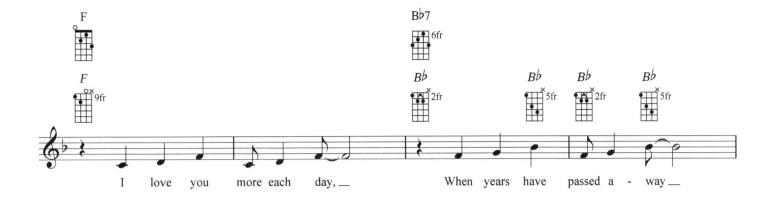

I love you more each day, __ When years have passed a - way __

you'll find my love be - longs __ to you on - ly.

'Cause when the world seems wrong, __ I know that I be - long, __

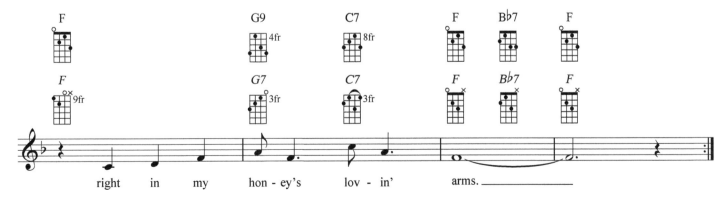

right in my hon - ey's lov - in' arms. _____

My Baby Just Cares For Me

from WHOOPEE!
Lyrics by Gus Kahn
Music by Walter Donaldson

My ba - by don't care for rings or oth - er ex - pen - sive things.

She's sen - si - ble as can be.

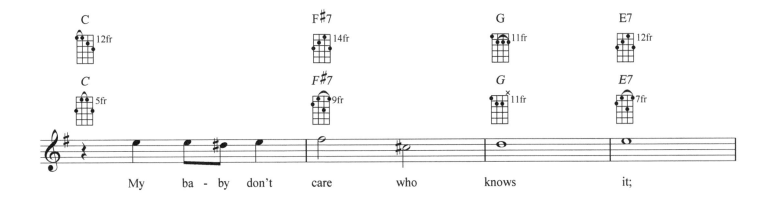

My ba - by don't care who knows it;

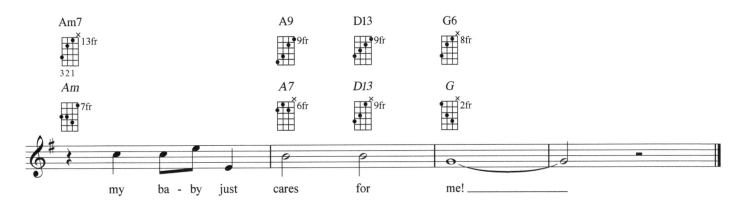

my ba - by just cares for me!

My Blue Heaven

Lyric by George Whiting
Music by Walter Donaldson

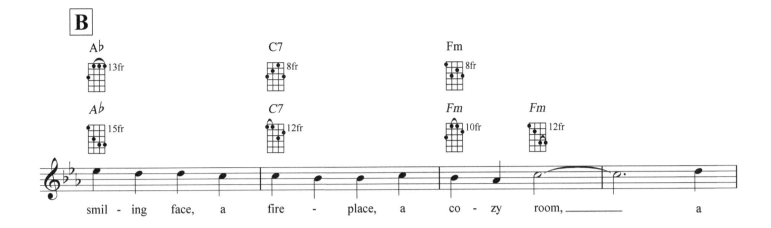

smil - ing face, a fire - place, a co - zy room, _____ a

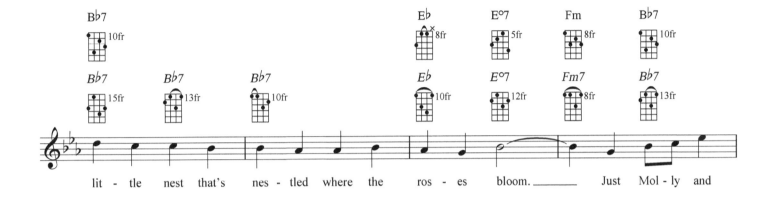

lit - tle nest that's nes - tled where the ros - es bloom. _____ Just Mol - ly and

me, _____ and ba - by makes three. _____ We're hap - py in

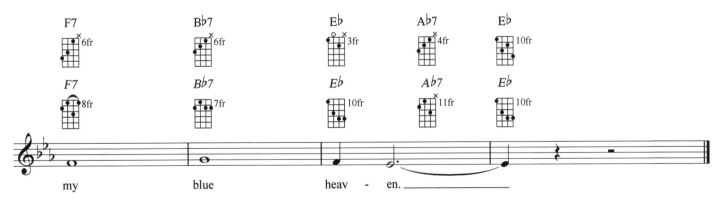

my blue heav - en. _____

Original Dixieland One-Step

Lyric by J. Russel Robinson and George Crandall
Music by D.J. (Nick) Larocco

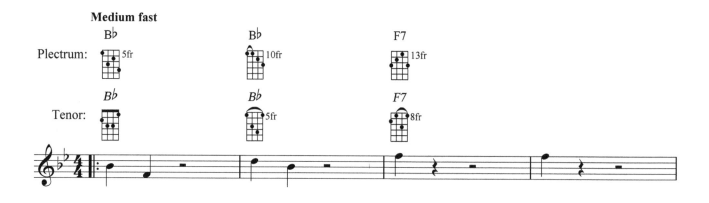

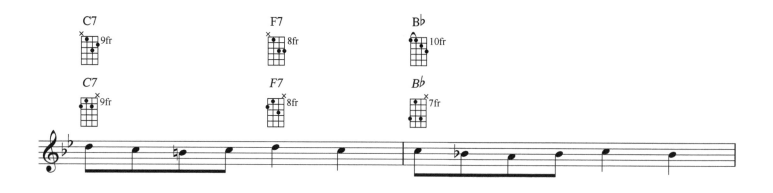

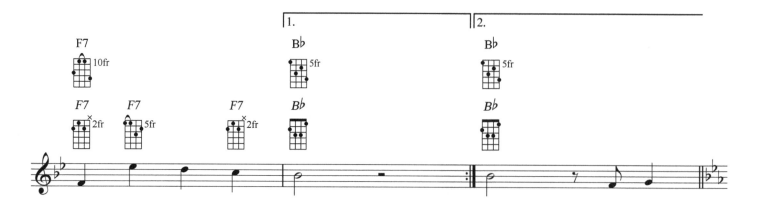

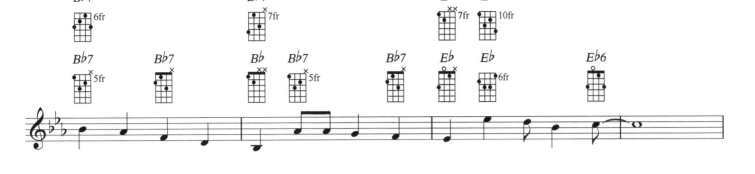

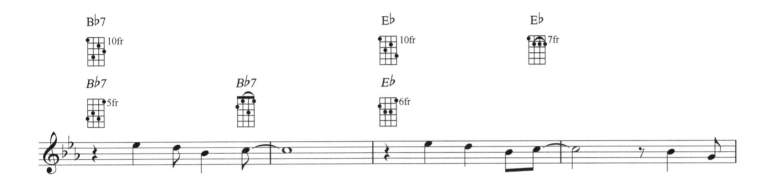

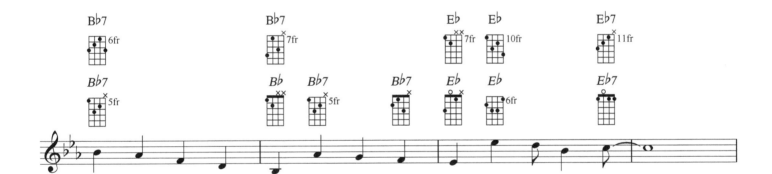

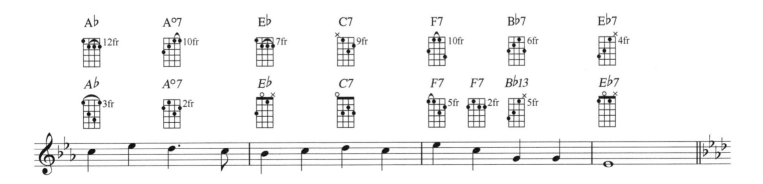

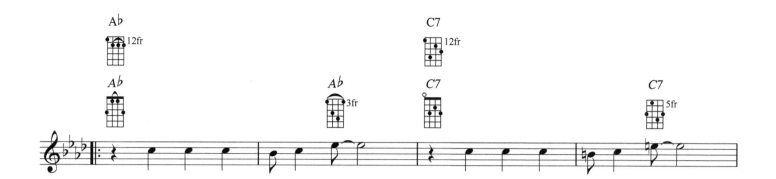

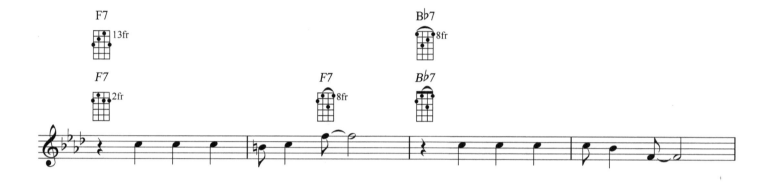

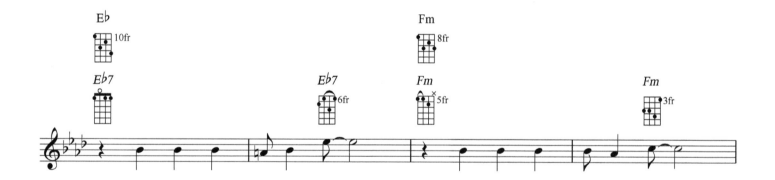

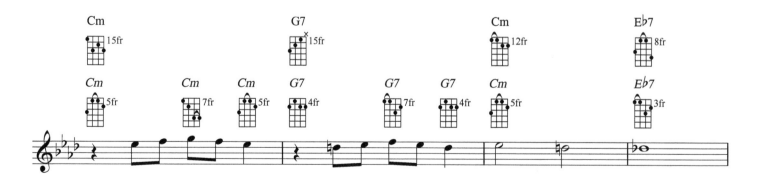

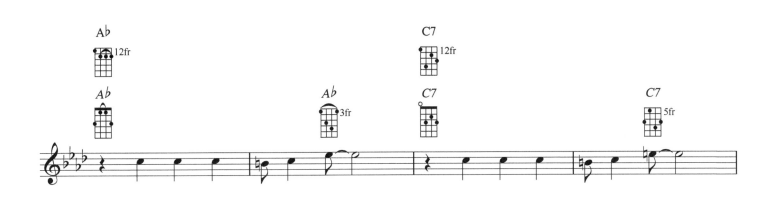

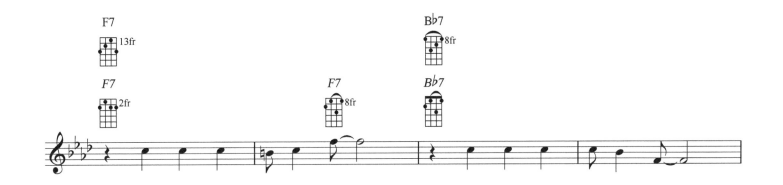

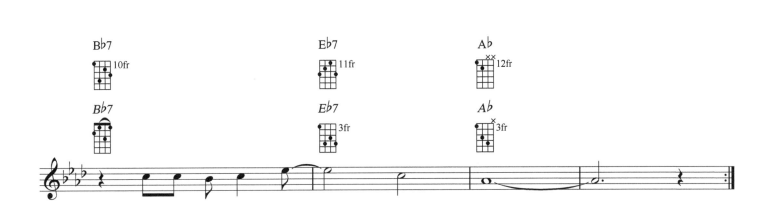

Royal Garden Blues

Words and Music by Clarence Williams and Spencer Williams

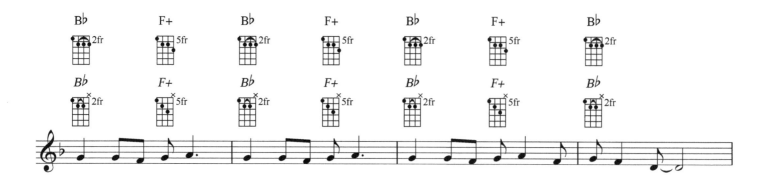

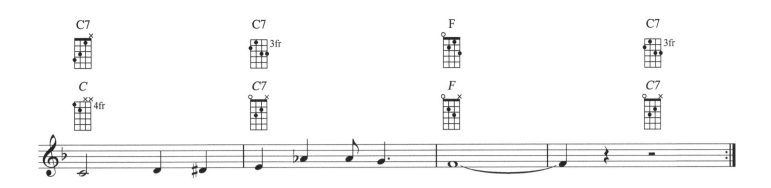

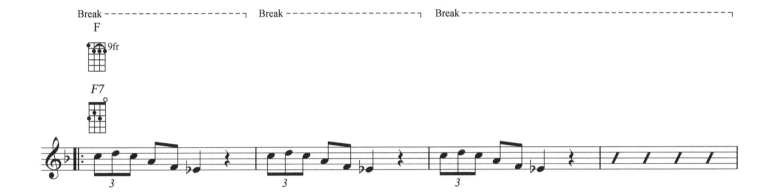

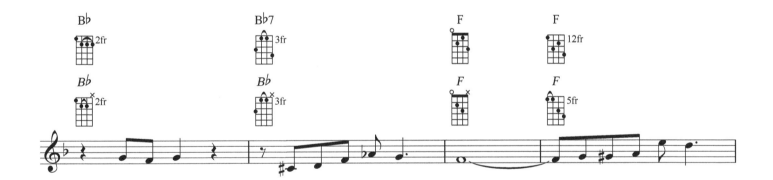

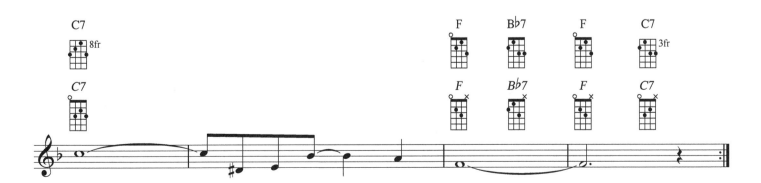

Dogfight

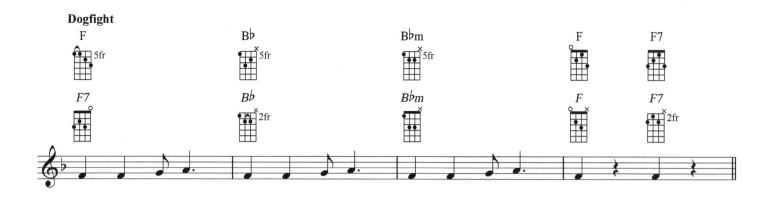

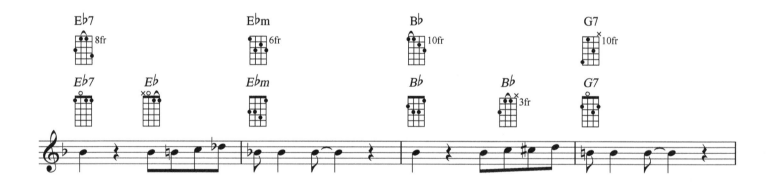

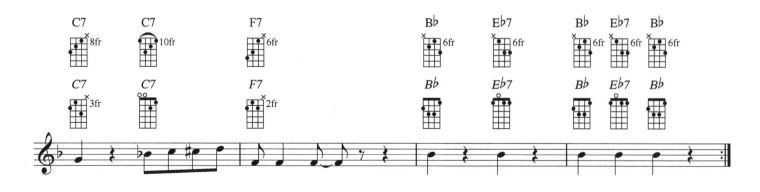

94

Struttin' with Some Barbecue

Words and Music by Lillian Hardin Armstrong and Don Raye

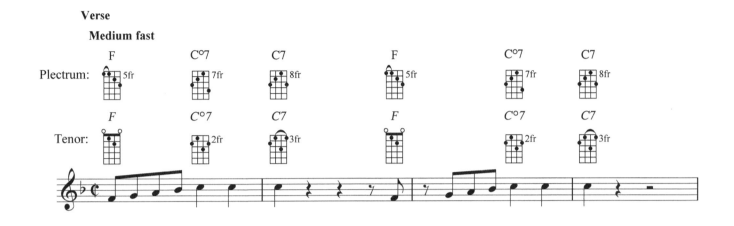

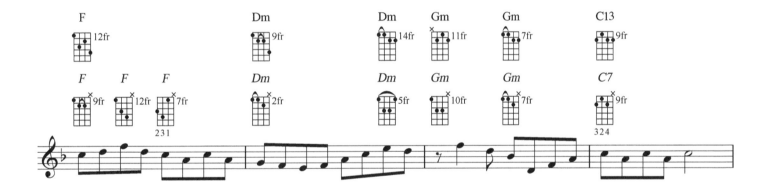

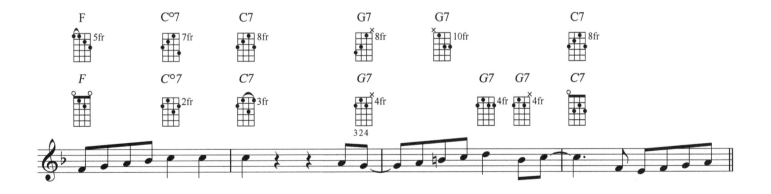

Chorus

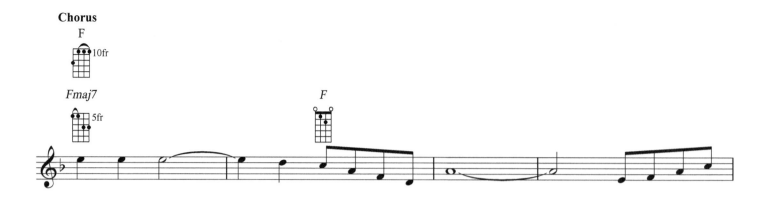

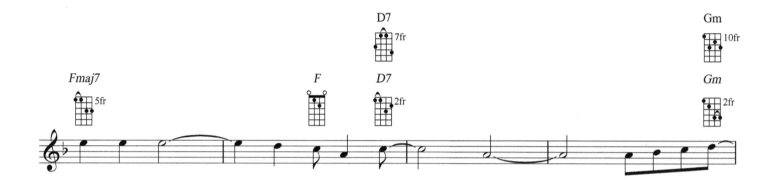

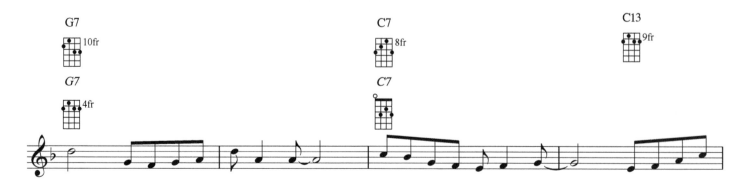

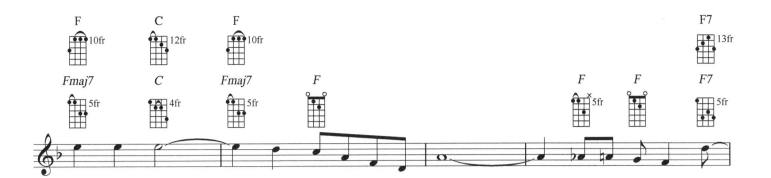

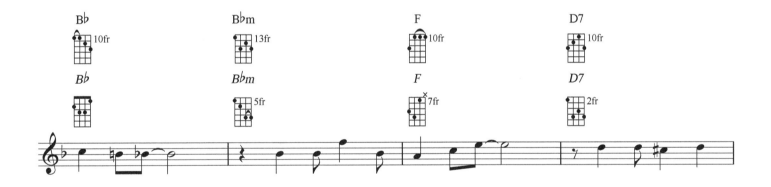

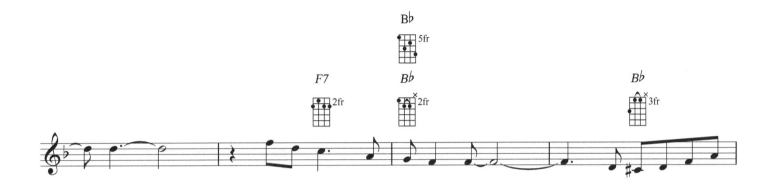

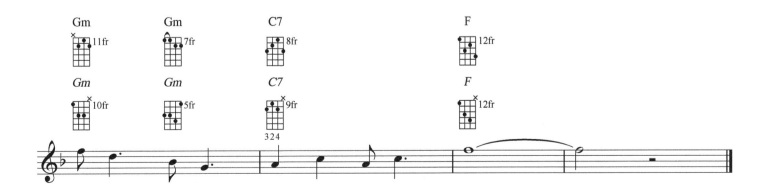

St. Louis Blues

from BIRTH OF THE BLUES
Words and Music by W.C. Handy

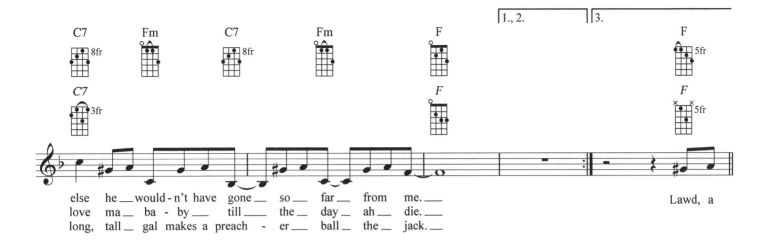

else he __ would-n't have gone __ so __ far __ from me.
love ma __ ba - by __ till __ the __ day __ ah __ die.
long, tall __ gal makes a preach - er __ ball __ the __ jack. __

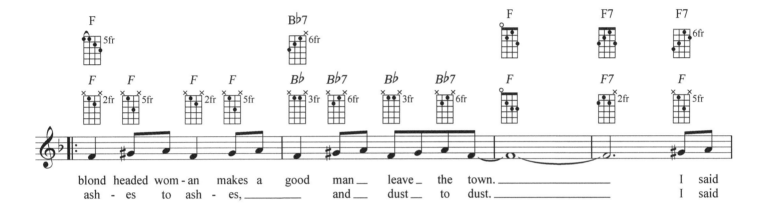

blond headed wom-an makes a good man __ leave __ the town. _____ I said
ash - es to ash - es, _____ and __ dust __ to dust. _____ I said

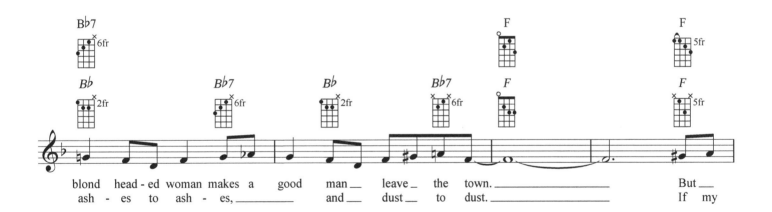

blond head-ed woman makes a good man __ leave __ the town. _____ But __
ash - es to ash - es, _____ and __ dust __ to dust. _____ If my

red - head - ed woman makes a boy __ slap his pa - pa __ down. __
blues don't __ get you, _____ my __ jazz - ing __ must. __

Some of These Days

Words and Music by Shelton Brooks

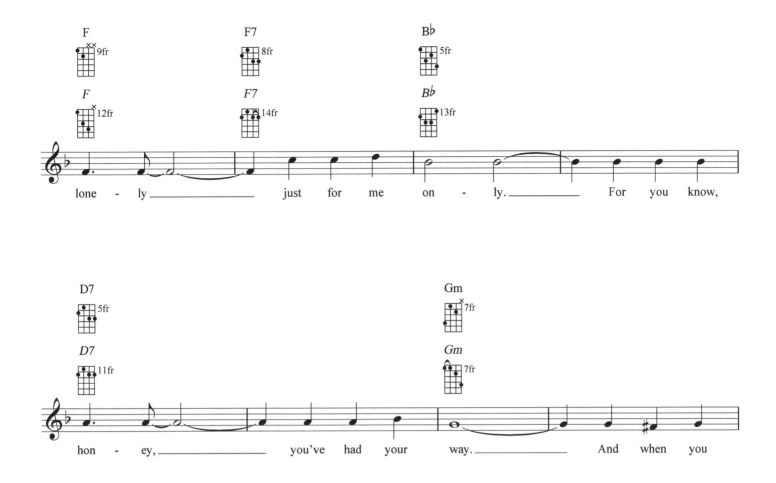

lone - ly _____ just for me on - ly. _____ For you know,

hon - ey, _____ you've had your way. _____ And when you

leave me, _____ you know you'll grieve me. _____ You'll miss _ your lit - tle

Fine   *D.S. al Fine*

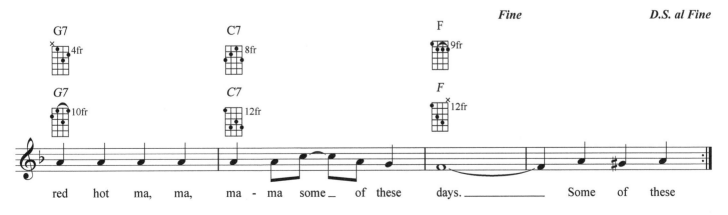

red hot ma, ma, ma - ma some _ of these days. _____ Some of these

Somebody Stole My Gal

Words and Music by Leo Wood

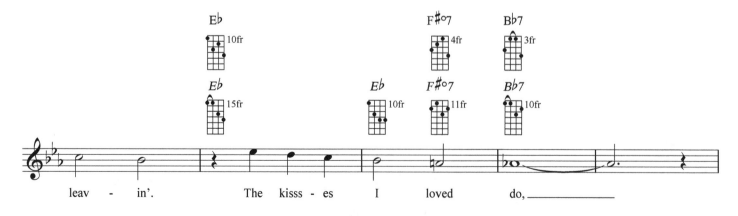

Stompin' at the Savoy

Words by Andy Razaf
Music by Benny Goodman, Edgar Sampson and Chick Webb

How my heart is sing - in', _____ while the band is swing - in', _____

*Plectrum *8vb*

nev - er tired of romp - in' _____ and stomp - in' with you, _ at the Sa - voy. _ What joy! _

**Plectrum *loco*

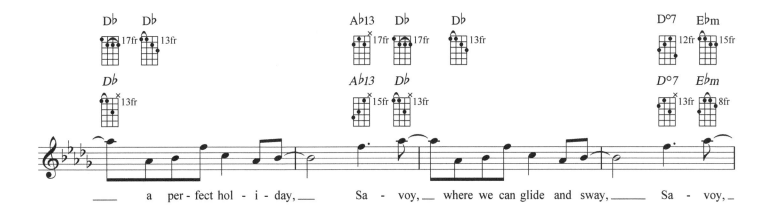

_____ a per - fect hol - i - day, _ Sa - voy, _ where we can glide and sway, _____ Sa - voy, _

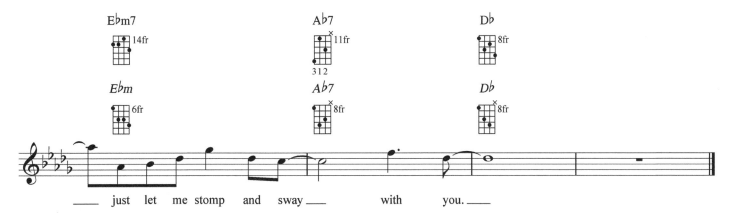

_____ just let me stomp and sway ___ with you. ___

Summertime

from PORGY AND BESS ®

Music and Lyrics by George Gershwin, DuBose and Dorothy Heyward and Ira Gershwin

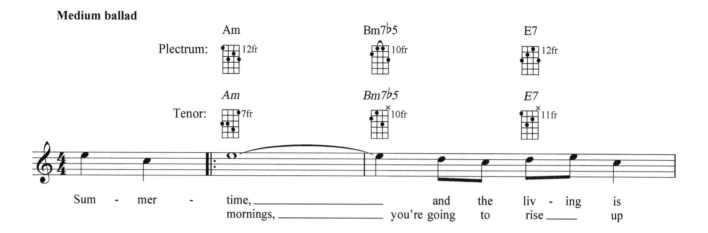

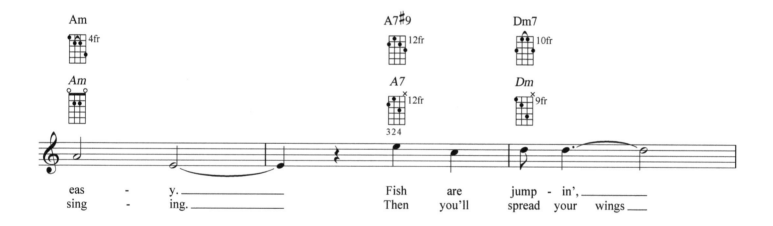

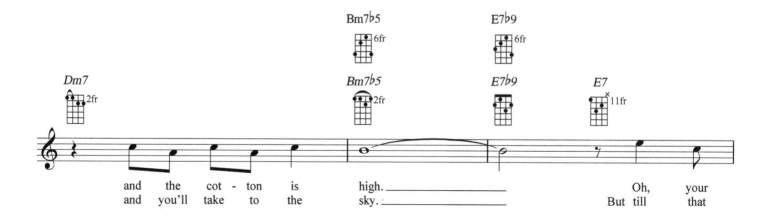

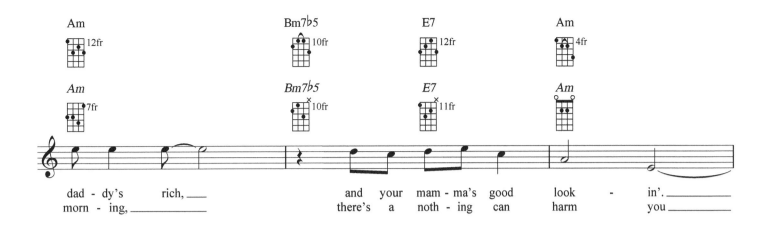

dad - dy's rich, _____ and your mam - ma's good look - in'. _____
morn - ing, _____ there's a noth - ing can harm you _____

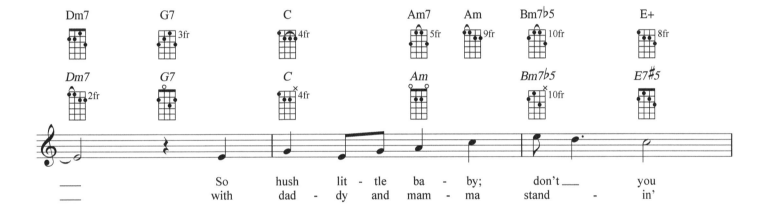

___ So hush lit - tle ba - by; don't ___ you
___ with dad - dy and mam - ma stand - in'

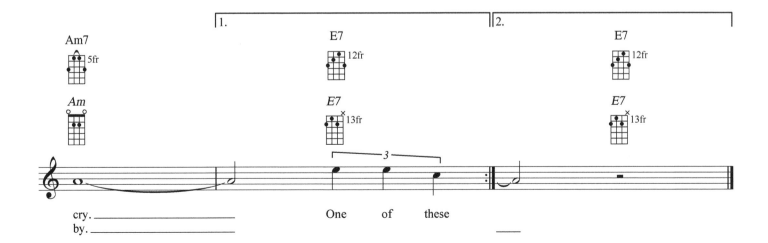

cry. _____ One of these
by. _____

Sweet Georgia Brown

Words and Music by Ben Bernie, Maceo Pinkard and Kenneth Casey

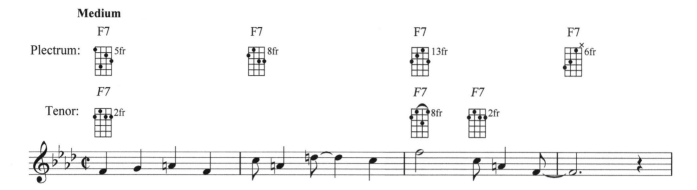

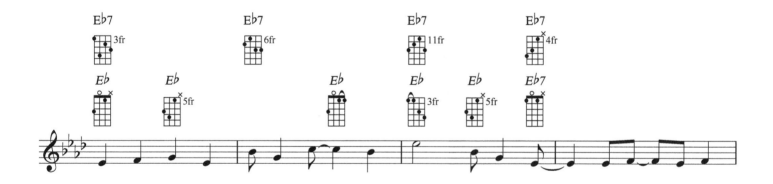

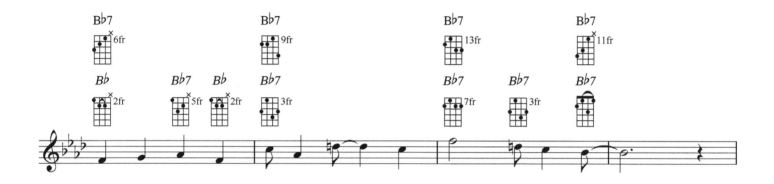

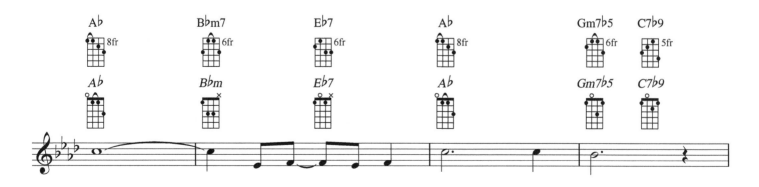

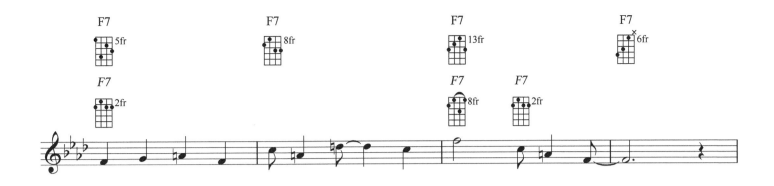

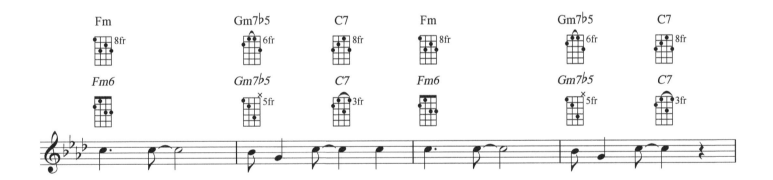

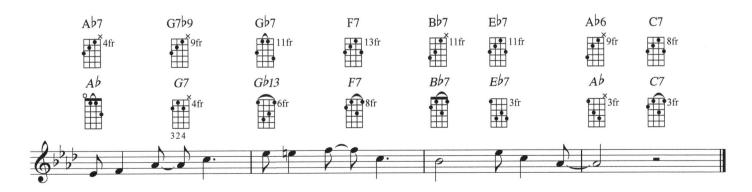

'Way Down Yonder In New Orleans

Words and Music by Henry Creamer and J. Turner Layton

The World is Waiting for the Sunrise

Words by Eugene Lockhart
Music by Ernest Seitz

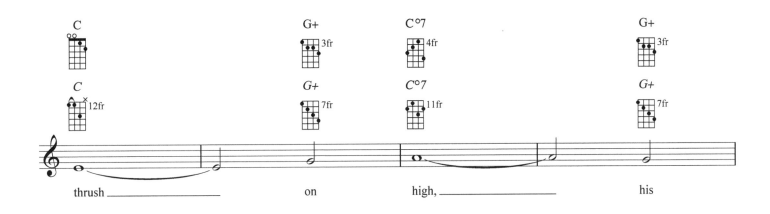

thrush _____ on high, _____ his

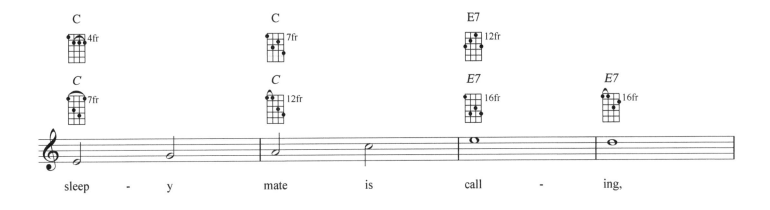

sleep - y mate is call - ing,

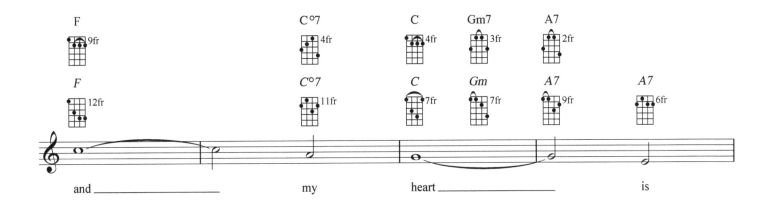

and _____ my heart _____ is

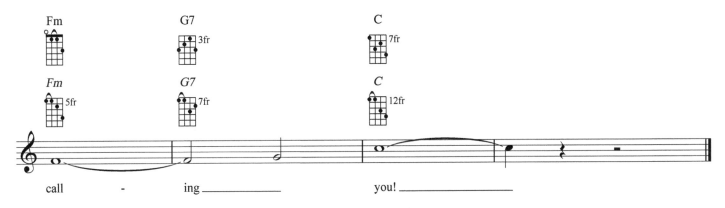

call - ing _____ you! _____

Yes Sir, That's My Baby

Lyrics by Gus Kahn
Music by Walter Donaldson

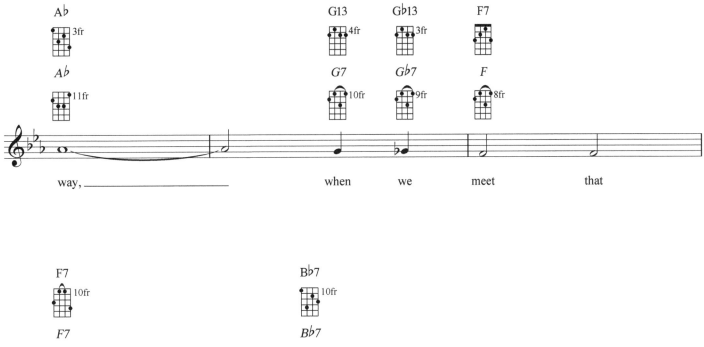

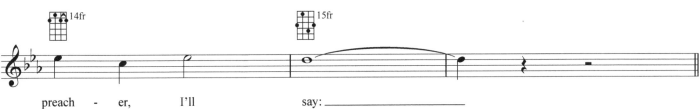

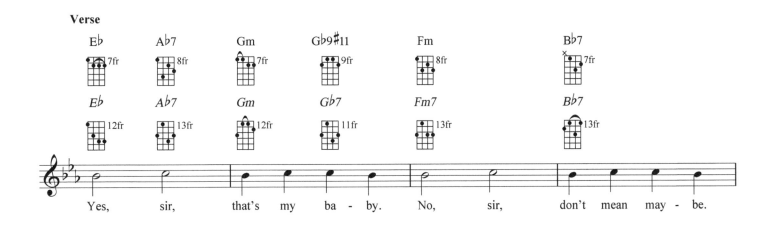

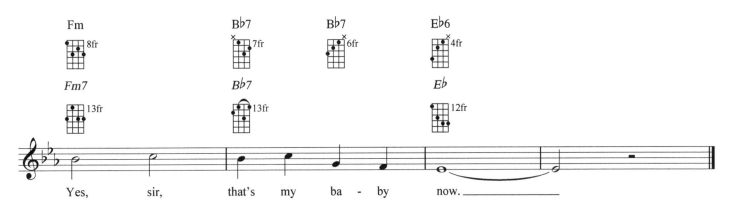

That's a Plenty

Words by Ray Gilbert
Music by Lew Pollack

rem - e - dy. _____ And that's a plen - ty, ___ plen - ty, plen - ty for me. ___

___

Once you start, you're gon - na stay ___ in it.
in the mood, there ain't no stop - pin' it.

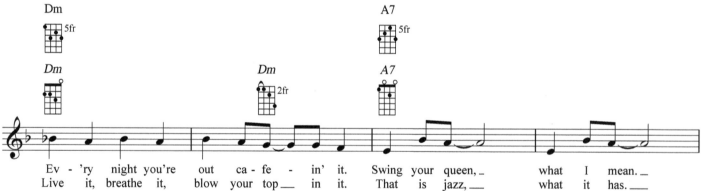

Ev - 'ry night you're out ca - fe - in' it. Swing your queen, _ what I mean. _
Live it, breathe it, blow your top ___ in it. That is jazz, _ what it has. ___

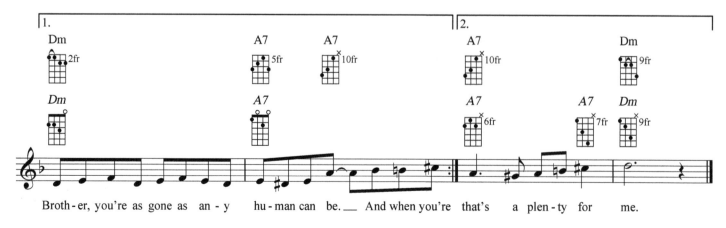

Broth - er, you're as gone as an - y hu - man can be. ___ And when you're that's a plen - ty for me.